A Detailed Seville, Spain Visitor Guide

Charlotte S. Richardson

All rights reserved. Copyright © 2023 Charlotte S. Richardson

COPYRIGHT © 2023 Charlotte S. Richardson

All rights reserved.

No part of this book must be reproduced, stored in a retrieval system, or shared by any means, electronic, mechanical, photocopying, recording, or otherwise, without written permission from the publisher.

Every precaution has been taken in the preparation of this book; still the publisher and author assume no responsibility for errors or omissions. Nor do they assume any liability for damages resulting from the use of the information contained herein.

Legal Notice:

This book is copyright protected and is only meant for your individual use. You are not allowed to amend, distribute, sell, use, quote or paraphrase any of its part without the written consent of the author or publisher.

Introduction

Welcome to this book, your passport to discovering the heart and soul of this enchanting city. Seville, the capital of Andalusia, Spain, is a place where history, culture, and gastronomy converge to create an unforgettable experience. In this guide, we'll take you on a journey through the city's most iconic landmarks, hidden cultural gems, culinary delights, and vibrant flamenco scene.

Seville is a city steeped in history, and its landmarks tell tales of centuries past. From the awe-inspiring Seville Cathedral to the majestic Alcazar Palace, we'll guide you through these architectural marvels and provide insights into their significance.

But Seville isn't just about its landmarks; it's a city with a rich cultural tapestry. We'll introduce you to the lesser-known cultural interest sites that locals hold dear. Explore charming neighborhoods, discover local traditions, and immerse yourself in Seville's authentic spirit.

No visit to Seville is complete without indulging in its world-famous cuisine. The city is a food lover's paradise, and we'll lead you to tapas bars where you can savor traditional Andalusian flavors. If you're on a budget, we've got you covered with affordable dining options. For those seeking a modern twist on Spanish cuisine, we'll point you toward innovative culinary experiences. And if you're after a truly exquisite meal, we'll reveal Seville's establishments that uphold the highest gastronomic standards.

Flamenco, an art form deeply intertwined with Andalusian culture, comes alive in Seville. We'll take you on a journey through the city's neighborhoods, where you can witness authentic flamenco performances among the locals. Whether you're in the historic Triana district or the bustling city center, you'll have the chance to experience the raw emotion and captivating rhythms of flamenco.

Beyond the city limits, Seville offers captivating destinations waiting to be explored. We'll provide recommendations for day trips and excursions, allowing you to discover the beauty of Andalusia's countryside and historic towns.

As you embark on your Seville adventure, keep in mind that this guide is crafted by locals who have a deep love for their city. Our aim is to ensure that you have an enriching and authentic experience, whether you're wandering the cobbled streets of Seville's neighborhoods, savoring tapas, or losing yourself in the passionate world of flamenco.

Seville is a city of contrasts, where ancient traditions coexist with modern influences, and we invite you to embrace every facet of it. So, let's begin this journey together, uncovering the secrets, flavors, and rhythms of Seville, one page at a time. Your adventure awaits in this book.

Contents

LANDMARKS 1
CULTURAL INTEREST SITES 16
GASTRONOMICAL SEVILLE 84
   Tapas Bars and Traditional Cuisine 88
   Affordable Options 104
   Modern Cuisine 113
   High Standards 120
FLAMENCO AMONG LOCALS 133
   Triana 136
   City Centre 142
EXPLORING OUTSIDE SEVILLE 147
     On site 177

LANDMARKS

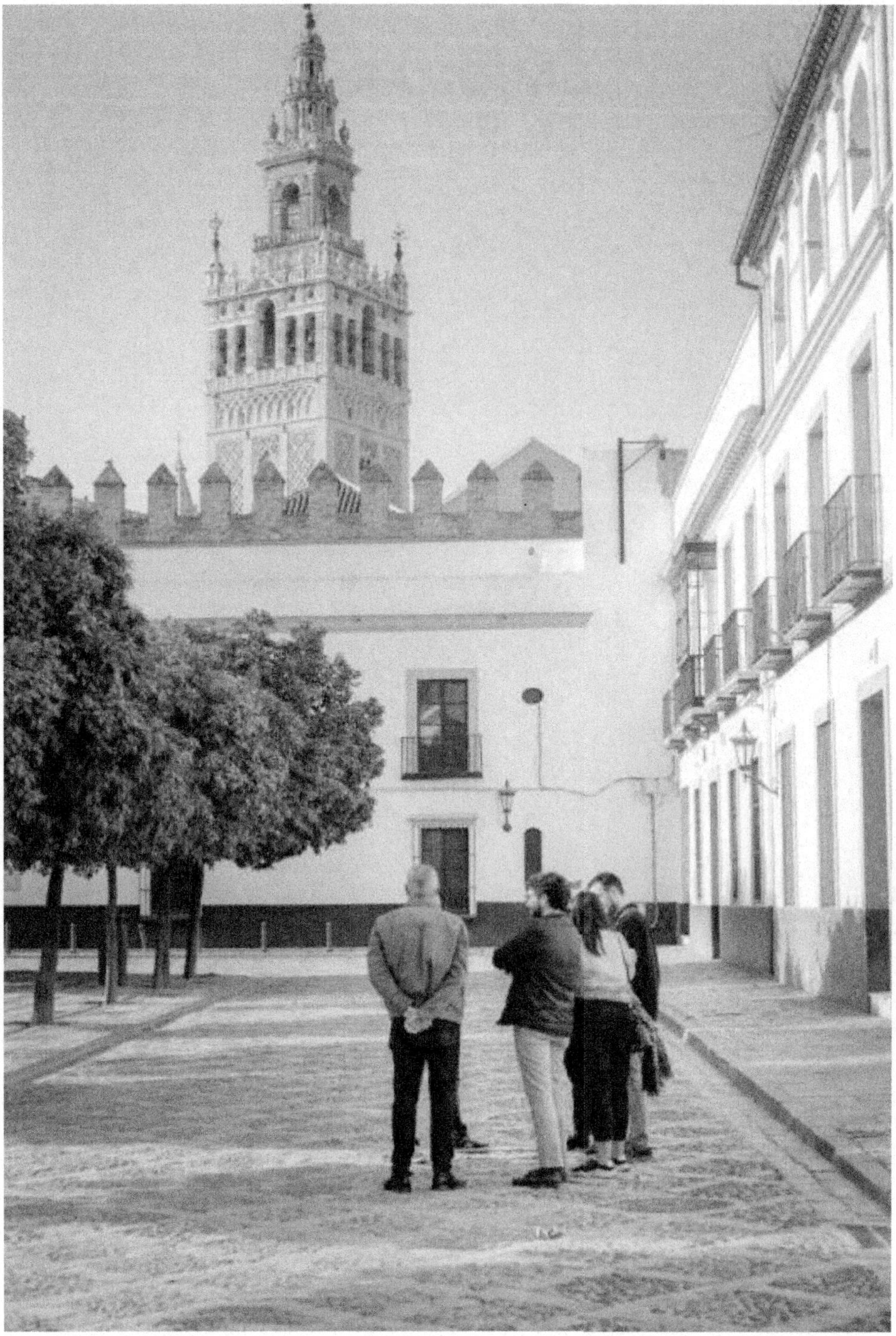

Real Alcázar de Sevilla

Address: Plaza del Triunfo / Patio de Banderas

Opening days: Every day (except 25th December, 1st & 6th January and Good Friday)

Visit times: April to September 9.30am–7pm
October to March 9.30am– 5pm

Ticket price: €13.50 (€14.50 if online) Extra €5.50 High Royal Room
Under 13 Free Entrance
EU students up to 30 years old €7

Website: www.alcazarsevilla.org

Audioguide: Available (€6)

Estimated time: 2 – 2.5 hours

Best time: Around lunch time

The Royal Alcázar of Seville is one of the three World Heritage listed monuments in the city and it is a truly unique landmark to visit. Alcázar, a word that is Arabic in origin, refers to palace, and here we will explore what is considered to be the oldest royal palace still in use in Europe.

The origins of this complex go back to the fortress built after the Norse Barbarians' invasion of the Moorish city of Seville in 844 AD. Since then, it has been the official residence of governors, rulers and kings.

We should approach our visit to the Alcázar open minded so that we can deeply immerse ourselves in the mixture of cultures, religions, patterns, materials and architecture styles within. In 12 centuries of history, many things have changed; yet all these changes are present in the Alcázar, from the decoration styles from different periods to the necessities demanded by the different rulers who lived there.

Seville was a Muslim city until 1248 AD, and the oldest part of the palace belongs to that period. What is really fascinating for the greater public, however, is the Mudéjar Palace: the new residence built in the 1360s by King Peter I of Castile and León.

Mudéjar was the name given to the Muslims who were allowed to stay in the area after the Christian conquest, and also refers to the style used by these Muslim artisans and workers at the service of Christian elites. Materials, patterns and even inscriptions will remind you of structures only found in Northern Africa or the Middle East, but these are considered Christian buildings. Peter I used this palace as his residence, so he also included the symbols of his kingdoms and religion, mixed with verses of the Quran.

The most impressive areas of the palace of Peter I are without doubt the Ambassadors' Hall and the Maidens' Courtyard. The first floor of the palace cannot be visited as it is reserved for the Spanish Royal family. Don't forget, this palace is still in use. Only the High Royal Room is opened with a special ticket.

Apart from the Mudejar Palace, it is also interesting to walk around the building of "Casa de la Contratación", the house of trade used for over two centuries as a logistics centre for everything regarding the new world. The Gothic Palace- the first Christian structure in the complex- and the magnificent gardens, including the bathrooms of María de Padilla, are also worth your time.

Indeed, these gardens and bathrooms, as well as the Ambassadors' Room of Peter I Palace, featured on the TV show, Game of Thrones. During the fifth season, the Alcázar was chosen as the Kingdom of Dorne. It was the perfect choice, as no special effects were required, and the set itself was already breathtaking.

Recommended Itinerary
- Hall of Justice and Plaster Palace
- Admiral's Room and Chapter House
- Peter I Palace
- Gothic Palace

- Maria Padilla Bathrooms
- Gardens:
  - Charles V Pavilion
  - Labyrinth
  - Grutesche Gallery

Tips & Info

It is highly recommended to book your tickets in advance if you want to skip the line and take advantage of every second in Seville. You can easily waste a whole morning queuing and it is not guaranteed that you will get inside. Once you have your tickets, purchased online (www.alcazarsevilla.org) or in the ticket office of Patio de Banderas, you can get inside the monument 15 minutes before and after the time shown on your ticket. The only entrance to the palace is *Puerta del León* (Lion's Gate) in Plaza del Triunfo.

Every ticket purchased for the Alcázar at the ticket office or online will have the name of the guest, as well as their ID or passport number. Please do not forget to bring the identification document you used to book your tickets with you on the day of the visit. Security staff will check your identity before letting you inside the complex. This is a new measure since May 2020, due to the increase of visitors in the complex reaching 2.2 million in 2019, and as an attempt to try and prevent reselling platforms charging a more expensive price for tickets to the monument.

Check the forecast before choosing your day to visit. It rarely happens, but please note that the gardens can be closed due to heavy storms and wind alerts. Although the gardens are very well looked after, this decision was made to prevent accidents.

If you have decided not to hire a private guide or join a guided tour, you can always rent your audio guide at the entrance for €6. I strongly recommend against visiting without a guide or source of information. Even if the place is beautiful to look at, you will miss a lot of relevant information if you do not have a guide.

Every Monday from 4pm, access to the Royal Alcázar is free. Please be aware that you cannot simply show up at the gate; you will still need to book your visit using the same online channel that you would use to get paid tickets.

Cathedral and Giralda Tower

Address: Plaza Virgen de los Reyes

Opening days: Every day (except 25th December, 1st & 6th January and Good Friday). **Please note that the cathedral is an active church and this calendar is subject to changes.**
Visit times: Monday to Saturday 10.45am– 6pm
Sundays 2.30pm – 7pm
Ticket price: €12 (€11 if online)
Under 14 Free Entrance
Students up to 25 years old €7 (€6 if online)
Website: www.catedraldesevilla.es
Audioguide: Available (€5)
Estimated time: 2 – 2.5 hours
Best time: Anytime

The Cathedral of *Santa María de la Sede* is a truly unique monument. Most people are used to visiting churches and cathedrals when they go to new places, but this seems to be from another world. The Cathedral of Seville is important because of two main facts; it is considered the largest cathedral in the world, and the original building at this location was actually a mosque, built at the end of the 1100s.

The new main mosque of Seville was finished by the Almohads in 1198, just between the city and the Alcázar, but only functioned as a mosque for 50 years.

In November 1248, the Christian troops of Castile, commanded by King Ferdinand III, ended the Muslim dominance of Seville after over 500 years. Since then, the same building has been a cathedral dedicated to the Virgin devotion of Santa María de la Sede. The sculpture of this Virgin of the XIII century is still preserved in the main altar of the cathedral.

Nowadays, only two parts of the previous mosque are preserved: the ablutions courtyard and the minaret. In the 1400s, the archbishop of Seville presented a project to build a new cathedral, following the Christian architecture style of the time. According to the tradition, the statement of the cathedral council was, *"Let us build a church so beautiful and so grand that those who see it finished will take us for mad"*.

The gothic building creates a rectangle of 126 x 83 metres, with over 30-metre-high naves. This magnificent Gothic structure was built occupying the previous prayer room of the mosque. Afterwards, new parts arrived in other styles: Renaissance, Baroque and Neoclassic.

Inside the cathedral, do not miss the main altar, which is considered the largest altarpiece in the whole of Christianity, with a Gothic wooden panel representing the most important scenes of the gospel.

The Giralda tower has been the symbol of Seville for over 800 years. You can see it from many parts of the city and enjoy its wonderful patterns and balconies. The tower was first built as a minaret of the previous mosque, and it is very similar to other Almohad minarets you find mainly in Morocco.

With the Christian arrival, the use of the tower changed and it became a bell tower. Now it has 24 different bells that still ring during important religious festivities.

You will have to climb 35 ramps to get to the bells' level on the Giralda. The reason that architect Ben Baso built this tower with ramps was to help the muezzin (the person who calls Muslims to prayer), who was using a donkey to get to the top of the tower. At the end of those 35 ramps, you will find 17 steps, built during the 1500s when Christians finished the top part of the Giralda in a Renaissance style. Up there, you will enjoy the best view of the city and you will be able to recognize the most iconic buildings of the

Seville skyline: the Alamillo Bridge, Pelli tower, 500th anniversary bridge, Plaza de España, Metropol Parasol and Torre del Oro.

Recommended Itinerary

- Patio de los Naranjos (courtyard)
- Main Altar & choir
- Silver Altar
- Chapel of Saint Anthony
- Chapel of Antigua
- Christopher Colombus' tomb
- Chalices' Sacristy
- Main Sacristy
- Chapter house
- Giralda tower

Tips & Info

The cathedral has a lot to see and you can stay inside the church as long as you want, as there will always be something to discover. The average visit should take about two hours, including the Giralda tower.

If have prepared yourself in advance with information, you might feel that you can explore on your own. If that is not the case, you can always hire a guide or rent the audio-visual guide.

Tickets can be purchased at the entrance that faces the Archive of the Indies (Puerta del Príncipe) and you can get inside directly. If you are visiting during peak season, you might see a long queue. There are two options to avoid it. The first is going to the Church of Divino Salvador. Most people do not know this, but the access to the cathedral includes the visit to this church. Once there, purchase tickets for both monuments (€12), visit the church and then head to the cathedral. There is another entrance exclusively used by those who have purchased tickets online, but it is also available to visitors with tickets bought at Salvador church. The name of this gate is

Puerta del lagarto (Lizard's Gate) and it is just at the base of the Giralda tower.

The other option, as with the Alcázar, is to purchase tickets online in advance (paying €1 admin fee less) and enter from the gate for online tickets visitors. If you enter from this gate and want to get an audio guide, you just need to head to the individual visitors' entrance, grab a map and ask anybody; the helpful staff of the cathedral will help you.

My recommendation would be to leave the Giralda tower to the end of the visit. Sometimes the way up can be slow as it is a narrow corridor for people going up and down. Do not rush, stay on your right and enjoy the view of the different balconies and small exhibitions in the middle rooms. Prepare yourself to listen to some of the bells once you are up there, as they will ring every 15 minutes.

The Royal Chapel of the cathedral cannot be visited from the interior of the church. This Renaissance chapel is dedicated to prayer and religious services take place there when the rest of the cathedral is open for cultural visits. There are other options to visit it though; from the gate facing Plaza Virgen de los Reyes, you will be able to enter every day from 10am to 2pm and from 4pm to 7pm.

The whole cathedral is also open for religious services every day in the morning. These services take place at different chapels depending on the day and the time. I highly recommend that you attend a Sunday service with organ music at the main altar at 10am.

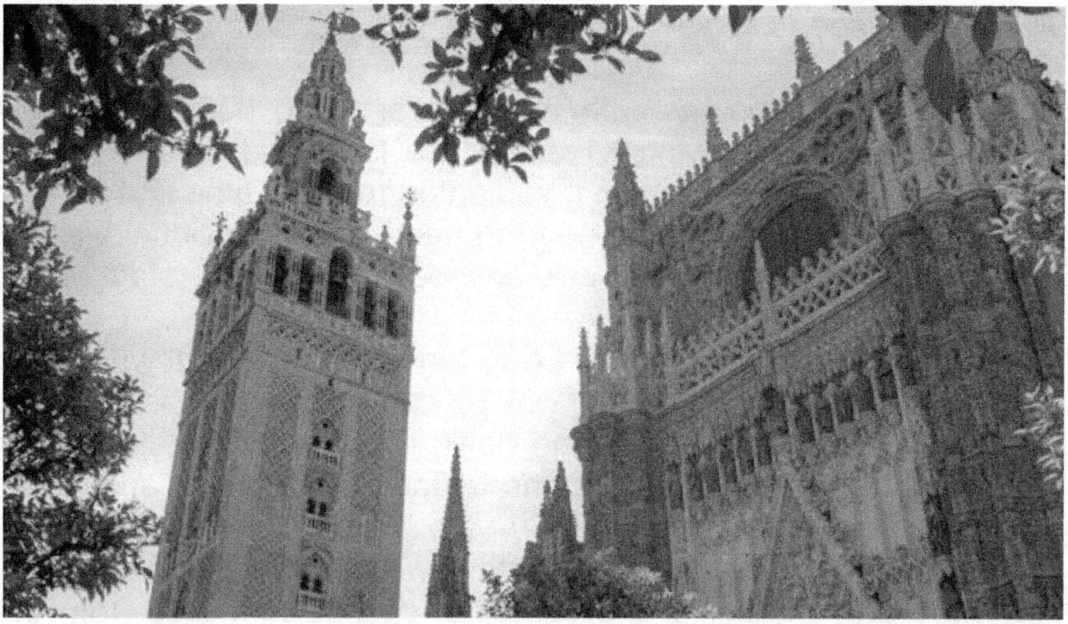

Plaza de España

Address: Avenida de Portugal
Opening days: Every day
Visit times: Monday to Saturday 8am– 10pm
Ticket price: Free access
Estimated time: 1 hour
Best time: Anytime

Plaza de España is one of the most iconic landmarks in Seville. Every visitor will take a picture in this site and as soon as you get there you will understand why. Although you have probably seen pictures of this monument, you will be impressed, as no one believes how massive it is.

At the beginning of the 20th century, Seville was getting ready to host one of the most important events in our history, the Ibero-American Expo of 1929. New boulevards were opened and every invited country started to build its pavilion to impress visitors and show its culture. Plaza de España was the pavilion of the host country of the Expo, Spain.

The architect chosen for the project was Aníbal González, and it perfectly represents the style of his time: *"regionalismo"*. Regionalismo consists of the mixture of elements of Moorish, Baroque and Renaissance revival styles of Spanish architecture.

Most of the countries invited had been former Spanish colonies and the shape of the building, a huge half circle, represents the hug of the mainland to those former territories. Around the square there is a moat with four bridges that represent the four ancient kingdoms of Spain: Castile, León, Navarra and Aragón. You will see benches around the buildings with the names of the provinces- one for each Spanish province- with a historical fact painted in amazing tile work and shelves at both sides. Plaza de España, as an open space, used to be a huge outdoor library. The buildings are still in use, as government offices and the General Captaincy of the Spanish army in Seville.

Plaza de España has also been converted in to a movie set several times, with films including Lawrence of Arabia and Star Wars shot here.

Tips & Info

To visit Plaza de España, you do not need a guide. It is enough to activate all your senses and just enjoy it. Plaza de España has a relaxed atmosphere; even if crowded, the place is too big to feel overwhelmed. A pleasant activity is rowing, with a boat rental service available around the moat. If you are in the mood for rowing, you can go for it for €6 (35 minutes).

Another way of spending your time would be simply walking around, listening to the guitar players or flamenco dancers and singers performing all over the square. You will also see some women trying to give you small branches of rosemary, but do not take it. They will say that it is only a gift, but they will ask you for money afterwards.

There are also many people selling *"typical Spanish"* souvenirs such as castanets, fans or shawls. Seville is a very safe city, but if there is a place where you should be more alert, that is Plaza de España. Sometimes the police are around advising visitors that there are pickpockets nearby, so please be careful and keep your belongings safe.

You cannot leave Plaza de España without going to one of the two balconies. Apart from the amazing staircases full of tiles, only from there will you really appreciate the dimensions of what you are looking at. On certain days, the central building is open to the public. If that is the case, it might be your lucky day and you will be able to visit the Theatre of Plaza de España, a hidden treasure for locals and visitors. As part of the Spanish army building, it only hosts some institutional events and small concerts.

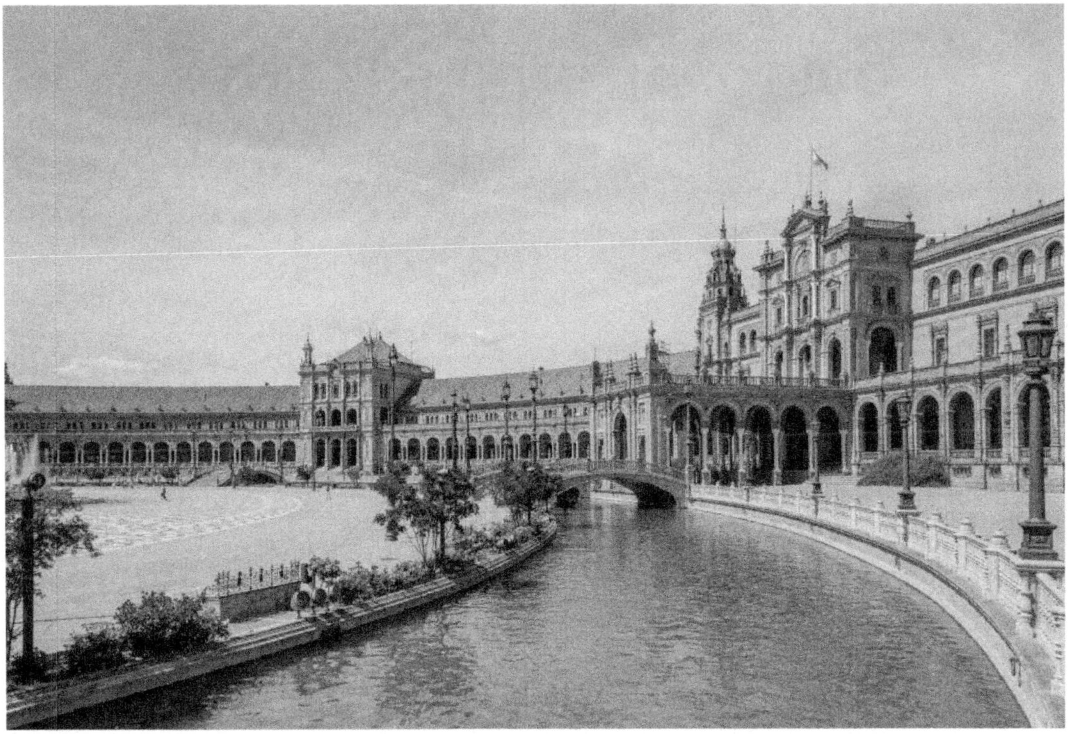

CULTURAL INTEREST SITES

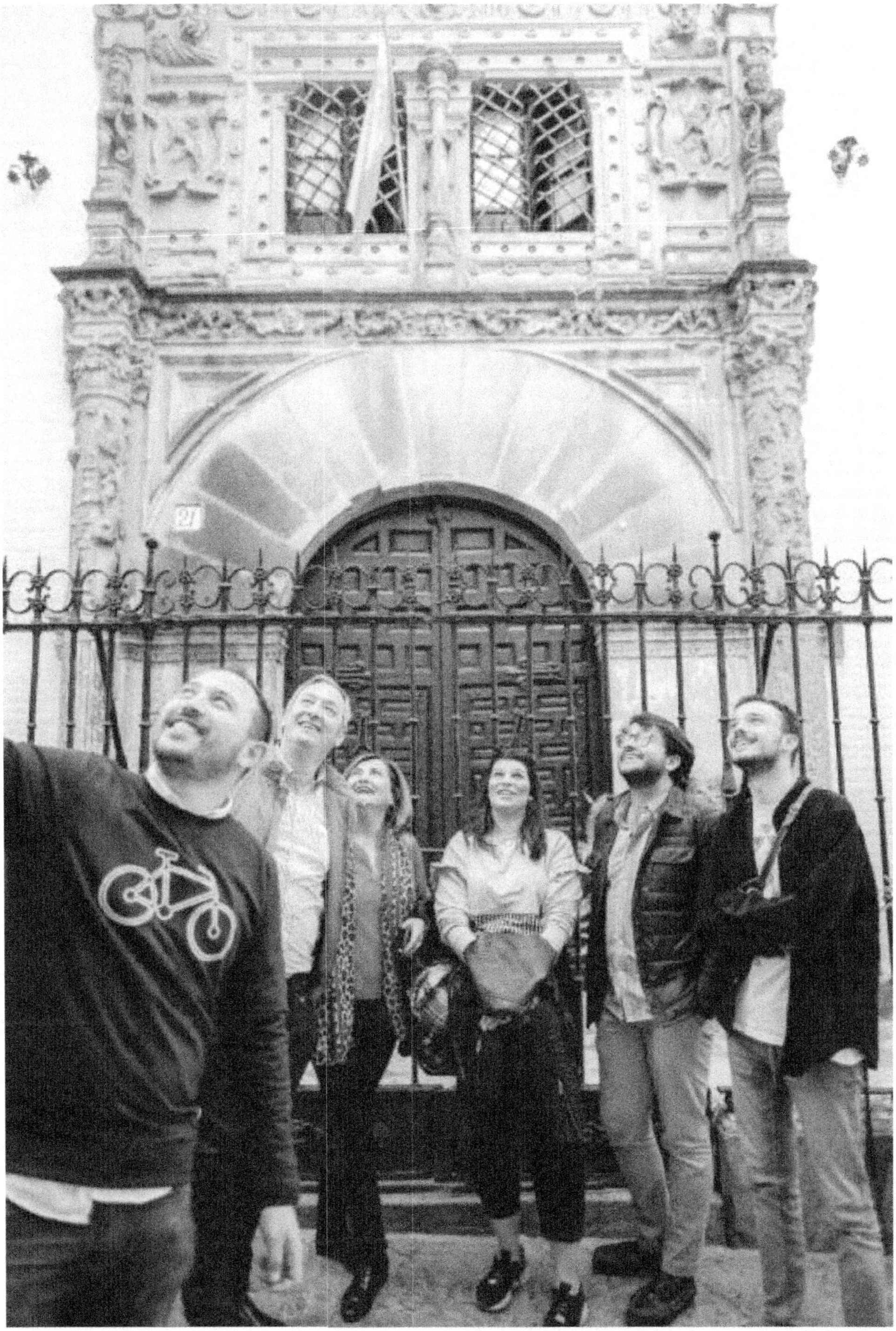

Casa de Pilatos

Address: Plaza de Pilatos, 1
Opening days: Every day
Visit times: April to October 9am – 7pm
November to March 9am – 6pm
Ticket price: €10 (ground floor) €12 (whole palace)
Audioguide: Included with the ticket
Estimated time: 1 – 1.5 hours
Best time: Anytime

Casa de Pilatos is the largest private palace in Seville and the second in general after the Royal Alcázar. It was built during the last quarter of the 15th century, after the union of the noble families of Enriquez and Ribera, two of the richest families in Andalusia.

The original palace was originally built in Mudéjar style with Gothic elements. The palace you can visit nowadays has lots of Renaissance style elements after refurbishments in the 16th century. These three styles are present in the main courtyard, one of the treasures of this noble house. During the 19th century, elements of Romanticism were also added, creating the atmosphere that visitors enjoy today.

Tips & Info

Casa de Pilatos is not always included in the general tourist routes around Seville, but it is really worth a visit. The name of the house has a curious origin, as it comes from Pilate, the Roman governor of the province of Judaea that ordered the crucifixion of Jesus. It is said that the distance between the chapel of this palace and the *Cruz del Campo* (Cross of the field) was the same as that between Pilate's house in Jerusalem and Calvary. That is how the tradition of the Holy Via Crucis and its 14 stations started to connect this house with the cross located outside the city walls, which is still standing. As you leave the palace and walk to San Esteban Street, you will see ceramic tiles on the walls representing the different steps of Jesus on his way to crucifixion.

It is very curious how this palace actually hosts two different houses; the ground floor as a summer residence and the first floor for the winter months. The first floor can be visited with guides from Casa de Pilatos, but pictures are not allowed. On the ground floor however, you can use the included audio guide and take all the pictures you want. Do not miss the staircase full of tiles and its dome that imitates the one in the Ambassadors' Hall of Peter I palace in the Alcázar. As with Plaza de España, Casa de Pilatos was also used as a set for Lawrence of Arabia, a cinematic masterpiece.

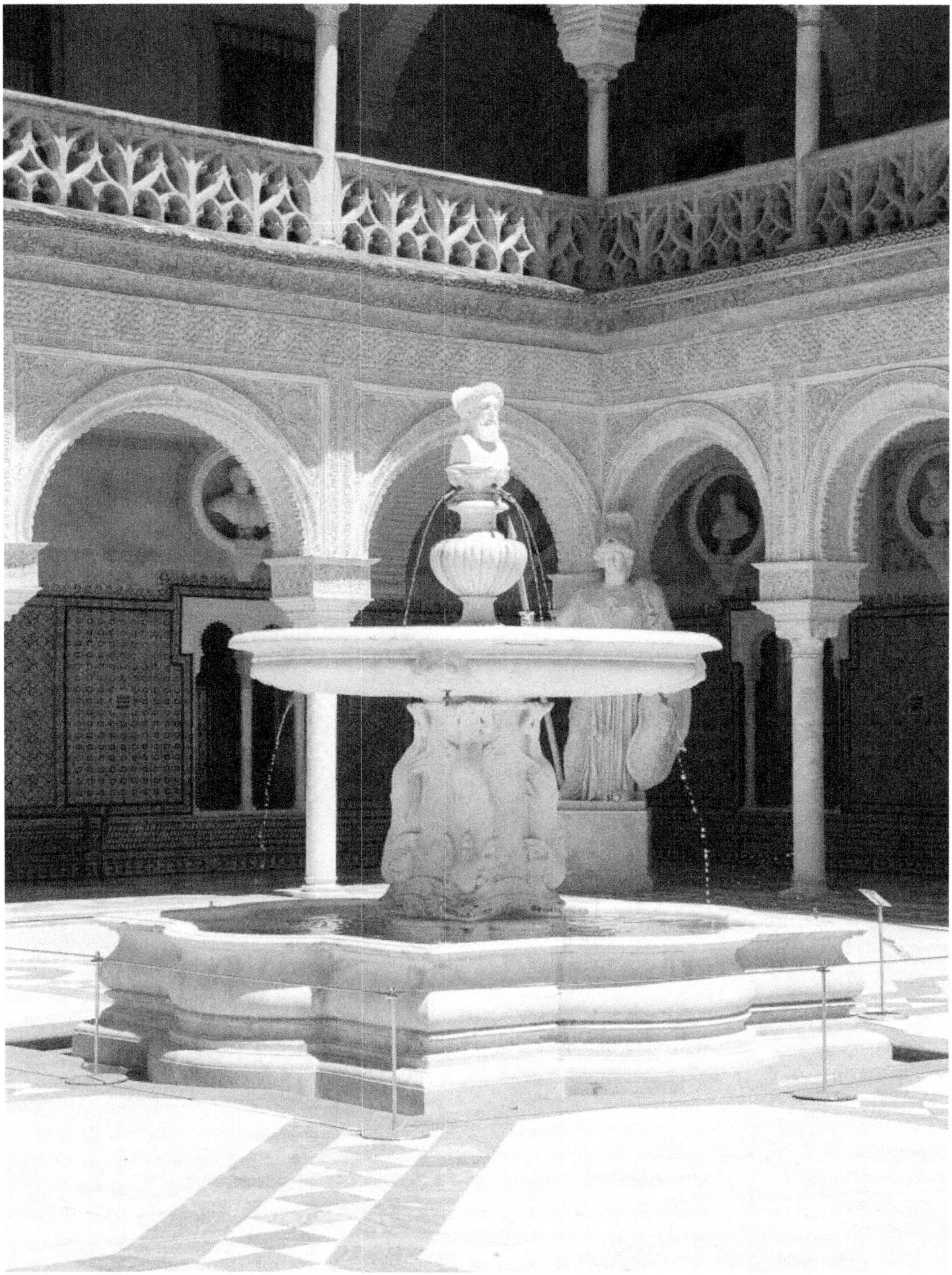

Palacio de las Dueñas

Address: Calle Dueñas, 5

Opening days: Every day (except 1st & 6th January and 25th December)

Visit times: April to September 10am – 8pm
October to March 10am – 6pm
Ticket price: €10 (Concession €8)
Audioguide: Available (€2)
Estimated time: 1 – 1.5 hours
Best time: Anytime

As with Casa de Pilatos, Palacio de las Dueñas was built by a noble family settled in Seville during the 15th and 16th centuries. It is the property of the house of Alba since 1612 and following the death of the last duchess in 2014, her son, the new duke, decided to open it to the public.

The house is a museum itself. In addition to the gorgeous architecture where Gothic, Mudéjar and Renaissance styles are combined, it hosts a private collection of archaeological remains and art. Paintings by masters such as José de Ribera decorate the private areas and tapestries and sculptures adorn every single hall of this house.

The house has two courtyards and four different gardens decorated with an exotic botanic collection.

Tips & Info

Only opened to the public in 2016, you should not miss the opportunity to visit Palacio de las Dueñas. You should not need more than one and a half hours. The audioguide can be rented at the ticket office for €2. If you prefer to use your phone and save some money, you can go to your app store and download the official app of Palacio de las Dueñas. With this, you will have all the information of the audio guide also written in your phone with images to recognize the different parts of the palace

The famous Spanish poet Antonio Machado was born in this palace in 1875. He was not part of the nobility, but during the second half of the 19th century, a lot of noble families decided to rent parts of their residences to middle-class families. The Machado family occupied one of the 12 apartments rented by the Duke of Alba.

Cayetana of Alba was one of the most important characters of Spanish society in the 20th century, as well as the most titled aristocrat in the world. She was an exception in aristocracy, with eccentric appearances in the media. Always surrounded by celebrities, some of them visited the palace on more than one occasion, such as Jackie Kennedy, Grace Kelly, Charlton Heston, Sophia Loren and Audrey Hepburn.

Palacio de la Condesa de Lebrija

Address: Calle Cuna, 8
Opening days: Every day (check for public holidays)
Visit times: 10.30am – 7.30pm
Ticket price: €12 (Children under 12 €6)
Audioguide: Not available
Estimated time: 1 hour
Best time: Anytime

The House of the Countess of Lebrija is not very well known for visitors that spend just a few days in Seville. This is another typical Andalusian noble family home built during the 1500s, but its interior is simply spectacular. With a predomination of the Renaissance style, the most decorative part of the palace is the central courtyard.

As you enter the courtyard, look down. Would it be possible to see Roman mosaics in a 16th century palace? In Seville it is. The Countess of Lebrija bought this noble house in 1901 and decided to decorate it in her own style, paving the ground floor with Roman mosaics originally from Italica, a Roman city just a few kilometres from Seville city centre. Lebrija palace now has the privilege of boasting what is considered the most expensive pavement at any European noble residence.

The plasterwork around the courtyard and some of the classic sculptures and busts in the patio are also impressive.

Tips & Info

You will find Palacio de la Condesa de Lebrija at the beginning of Cuna Street, and buy your tickets at the entrance.

The ground floor can be explored by yourself; spend all the time you want admiring the pavements. To visit the first floor, you need to wait for the guided tour, and as you will go around the private part of the house, it is not allowed to take pictures. This is probably because the heirs of the countess left that floor as it was during the time they lived there and they want to keep the privacy of the family.

The main point of interest about this palace regards the mosaics. How was it possible to move such rich heritage from its original location? We know that the Countess was passionate about archaeology and art and apart from her family heritage, she dedicated part of her life to collecting new pieces for her private collection. The official version of events says that these mosaics were in her lands and then were moved to her residence.

Las Setas de Sevilla (The Mushrooms)

Address: Plaza de la Encarnación
Opening days: Viewpoint: Every day
Antiquarium: Tuesday to Sunday
Visit times: Viewpoint: 9.30am – 12am
Antiquarium: 11am – 8pm
Ticket price: Viewpoint day €5/ Viewpoint night €10 Feeling Sevilla €5/ Antiquarium: €2.10
Audioguide: Download mobile APP
Estimated time: 1.5 hours for both
Best time: Sunset

Las Setas is the most modern cultural interest site included in this book. Cities like Seville seem to be living in the past, but with this project, Seville city centre takes a leap into the 21st century.

It was built by the German architect Juergen Mayer between 2005 and 2011. The design is in total contrast to most of the architecture of Seville city centre, but it offers something completely different to visitors and locals and has helped to develop that area of the city.

Underneath the Parasol structure we can visit the Antiquarium of Seville, the most important Roman archaeological site in the city. It was discovered in the 1990s during an attempt to open an underground car park, opening to the public in 2011.

Tips & Info

The first thing you should know about this building is that even if it was named Metropol Parasol, it was renamed as *Las Setas*. Setas is the Spanish word for mushroom, much easier to recognise by locals because of its shape.

Las Setas has always been a controversial building since the project was approved. Architecture has been evolving and Seville city centre has stayed immovable for centuries. A part of the city society rejected this project due to its modernity, but just after the building was opened, locals started to feel it as their own. The controversy did not finish there, as the cost of the project tripled, reaching €100 million. On its 10th anniversary, in 2021 the building transformed including an audiovisual and sensory space (Feeling Sevilla) and night lights shows known as Aurora.

Going along the walkway of the viewpoint is a must while in Seville, even better if around sunset. The view from Las Setas is better than the one from the Giralda, as you will see the tower from here.

The Antiquarium is also an interesting visit, with very well-preserved Roman mosaics. The only pity is the lack of information, so you will have to deal with panels.

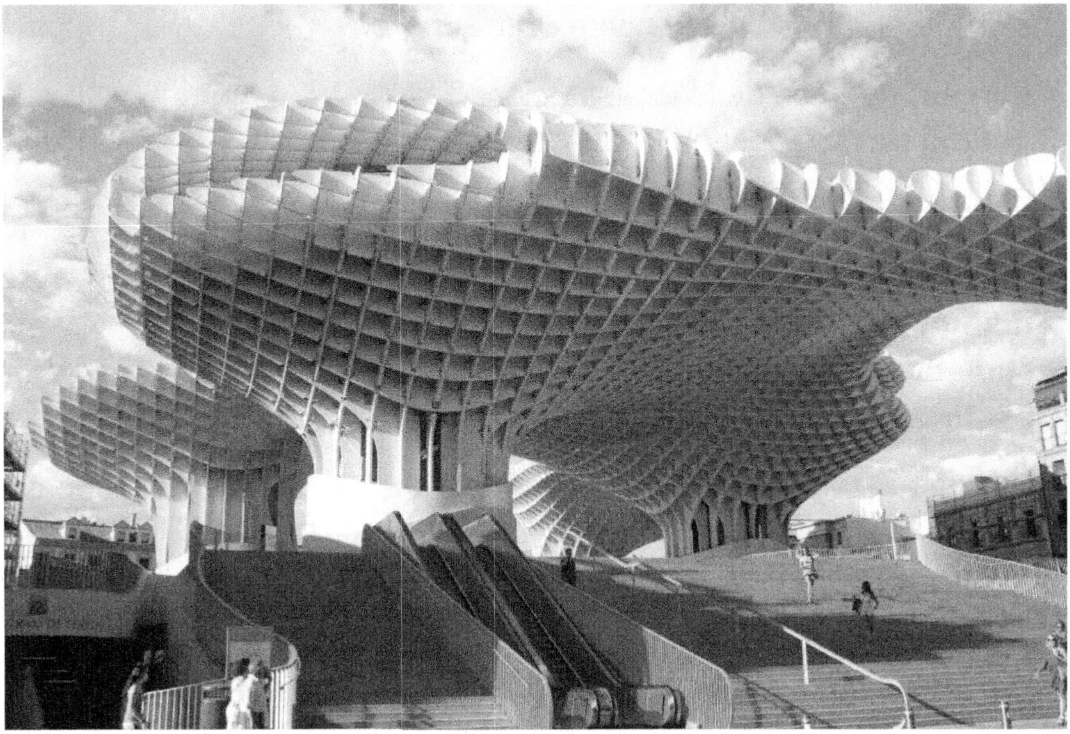

Archive of the Indies

Address: Avenida de la Constitución, 3
Opening days: Tuesday to Sunday
Visit times: Tuesday to Friday 9.30am – 5pm
Sat 9.30am – 8pm Sunday 10am – 2pm
Ticket price: Free access
Audioguide: Not available
Estimated time: 45 minutes
Best time: Anytime

Together with the Real Alcázar and the Cathedral, the General Archive of the Indies was included in the Unesco World Heritage list in 1987. The origin of the building dates to 1572, when King Philip II commissioned it from architect Juan de Herrera with the objective of hosting the merchants' affairs. Seville was receiving all the ships coming from America and those products were sold in that building

The building worked as a house of trade until 1717, when *Casa de la Contratación* was moved to Cádiz. Seville was no longer the capital for trade with the New World and the building fell into disuse. In 1785 King Charles III ordered that the archives of the Council of the Indies should be kept here in Seville. Since that moment all the documentation regarding the overseas empire has been kept in this building.

Tips & Info

The General Archive of the Indies is a very interesting museum, which helps us immerse ourselves in the city of the 16th and 17th centuries. Just steps away from the cathedral and the Alcazar you cannot pass by without entering and having a look.

The building itself is beautiful, designed by the same architect behind the monastery of El Escorial, and very similar in its shape, with a central patio.

The building, as well as the cathedral, is surrounded by columns connected with chains, originally to protect the business held inside the building. Casa de la Contratación was founded in 1503 and from the very beginning, merchants sold their products in the surroundings of the cathedral, so the first chains were placed around the church. On rainy days, business used to take place inside the church, until the cathedral council complained to the king, who ordered the building of this new merchants' house across the street.

Nowadays, the archive holds 43,000 files, with 80 million pages and 8,000 maps. These documents are not kept in the building itself, but at a more modern one across the street. These documents are in the process of being digitalized, but it will take time. If we placed all the documents, one on top of the other, we could create a mountain 8 kms high.

Bullring (Plaza de Toros)

Address: Paseo de Cristobal Colón, 12
Opening days: Every day
Visit times: Nov to March 9.30am – 7pm
April to Oct 9.30am – 9.30pm
Bullfight days 9.30am – 3pm
Ticket price: €10 (Concession €6)
Audioguide: Guided visit
Estimated time: 45 minutes – 1 hour
Best time: Anytime

Bullfights in Spain, as we know them today, have their origins in the 1700s, but the tradition of festivities involving bulls comes from the ancient age. *Real Maestranza de Caballería* is the name of the bullring in Seville. It was built during the 18th century, and is one of the oldest in Spain and the first ever built in a big city.

The bullring was built in late Baroque style in the *Arenal* neighbourhood, just between the old city walls and the Guadalquivir River. It hosts up to 11,000 fans of this sport during the bullfighting season, starting on Easter Sunday and running for three weeks until the end of the April Fair.

La Maestranza is considered one of the most prestigious bullrings in Spain due to the demanding jury and the most skilled bullfighters come to perform their art every year.

Tips & Info

The visit to the bullring in Seville is interesting even for those who have never heard of bullfighting before. The tour is led by a guide of the bullring, who will explain everything carefully so that you understand this art.

On your journey, you can visit the colourful arena where white, ocher and burgundy will mix in harmony. The most breathtaking part of the visit is the chapel of the bullfighters. There, most of the performers will have their time of prayer before getting into the ring and risking their lives. The bullring is also home to a museum with historical paintings as well as old costumes donated by famous bullfighters.

Lots of people wonder how bullfighting still continues in the 21st century. Some people defend it as a tradition, and others would want to abolish it because of animal cruelty. These bulls are prepared for bullfighting even before they are born, with the selection of the mothers, and are well looked after during the four years they live before the fight. Having said this, we cannot deny the pain the animal suffers during the 20 minutes of the performance until it dies.

If you are visiting Seville in June and are interested in attending a bullfight, there is an affordable option. For €10 you can go on Thursday evening to a *novillada,* where young bullfighters will perform, hoping to become professionals.

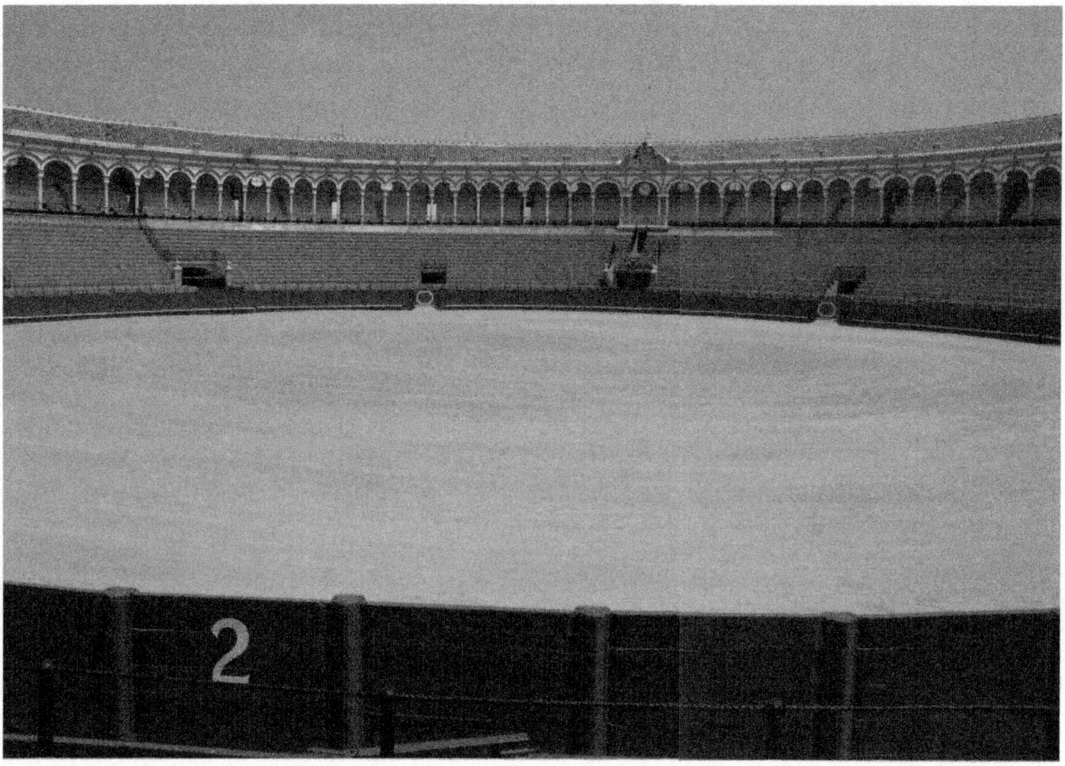
2

Triana Bridge

Address: Puente de Isabel II
Opening days: Every day
Visit times: All day (outdoors)
Ticket price: Free access
Audioguide: Not needed
Estimated time: 45 minutes
Best time: Sunset

Puente de Isabel II is the official name of this bridge that connects the city of Seville with the Triana suburb. It was built in the 19th century, finished in 1852 under the reign of Isabella II and taking her name.

The bridge was designed by two French engineers, Fernando Bernadet and Gustavo Steinacher, inspired by the Parisian bridge of Carrousel, which was demolished in 1930. The materials used in the Triana Bridge are iron and stone, with two double pillars of stone that support the weight of the whole structure.

On the Triana side of the bridge, the Chapel of Carmen is a must see. The Chapel of Carmen was built in 1928 by Anibal González, the same architect that designed Plaza de España in a regionalist style. In 1976, it was declared a National Historical Monument and it is one of the symbols of the city and Triana neighbourhood.

Tips & Info

The city of Seville has nine bridges that perfectly connect the different areas in an easy way, with the bridge of Isabel II the most important, because of its history and uniqueness.

Triana Bridge is one of the most iconic symbols of the city of Seville and it is very helpful in order to completely understand the history and geography of the city. Triana is the suburb across the river and an area linked to the city since Roman times. It was never surrounded by the city walls and its only connection with the old town was through a bridge.

Due to the difficulty in establishing firm foundations, old civilizations rejected the idea of building a solid bridge. In the 1100s, under the Moorish rule, a floating bridge consisting of boats was built to connect the city with the suburb of Triana. This was the only bridge existing from the 12th until the 19th century, when the modern iron bridge replaced it.

The view of the bridge is impressive from both shores. In Paseo de Cristobal Colón there is a lower pathway where you can go and contemplate the view as well as in Calle Betis on the Triana side.

Fine Arts Museum

Address: Plaza del Museo, 9
Opening days: Tuesday to Sunday
(check public holidays)
Visit times: September to July 9am - 9pm except for Sundays 9am – 3pm
August 9am – 3pm
Ticket price: €1.50 (Free for EU citizens)
Audioguide: Not available
Estimated time: 1 – 1.5 hours
Best time: Anytime

The Museum of Fine Arts is the most important collection of art in the whole city and hosts masterpieces from the medieval period to the early 20th century. It is considered the second richest gallery in Spain after Museo del Prado in Madrid. The museum was established in 1841 at an old convent that closed after the ecclesiastical confiscation of 1835. You can still see the patios and different rooms, as well as the church or the refectory, now part of the museum.

From the collection, painters that lived or worked in Seville stand out, the greatest being Murillo, Zurbarán, Valdés Leal or Herrera. These Baroque works are the proof of the greatness of the city during the 1600s and the spread of local artists and their techniques is a sign of the cultural importance of Seville.

Tips & Info

Despite the significance of the artists and paintings of the museum, this is a very quiet place with a relaxing atmosphere, out of the tourists' crowds. The exhibition rooms are distributed around the central courtyard, the former cloister of the monastery. There is no audioguide available, so even if you follow the information panels, it's worth considering buying any guide at the shop beside the ticket office.

The first four rooms are dedicated to Medieval and Renaissance art until the beginning of the 17th century. The essence of this museum though, is the work of the Baroque masters of the 17th century. In room five, the former church of the monastery, you will find the magnificent paintings of Murillo. Some of the paintings are displayed at the former altar imitating the composition Murillo painted for the Convent of Capuchinos of Seville. To find another great artist like Zurbarán, you will have to go to room 10 while Valdés Leal's works are displayed in room eight.

The Museum of Fine Arts of Seville is a very active institution, depending on the regional government of Andalusia. They organize many temporary exhibitions dedicated to a specific artist or movement that are usually very successful. If there is any exhibit on while you are staying in the city, do not hesitate and go for it.

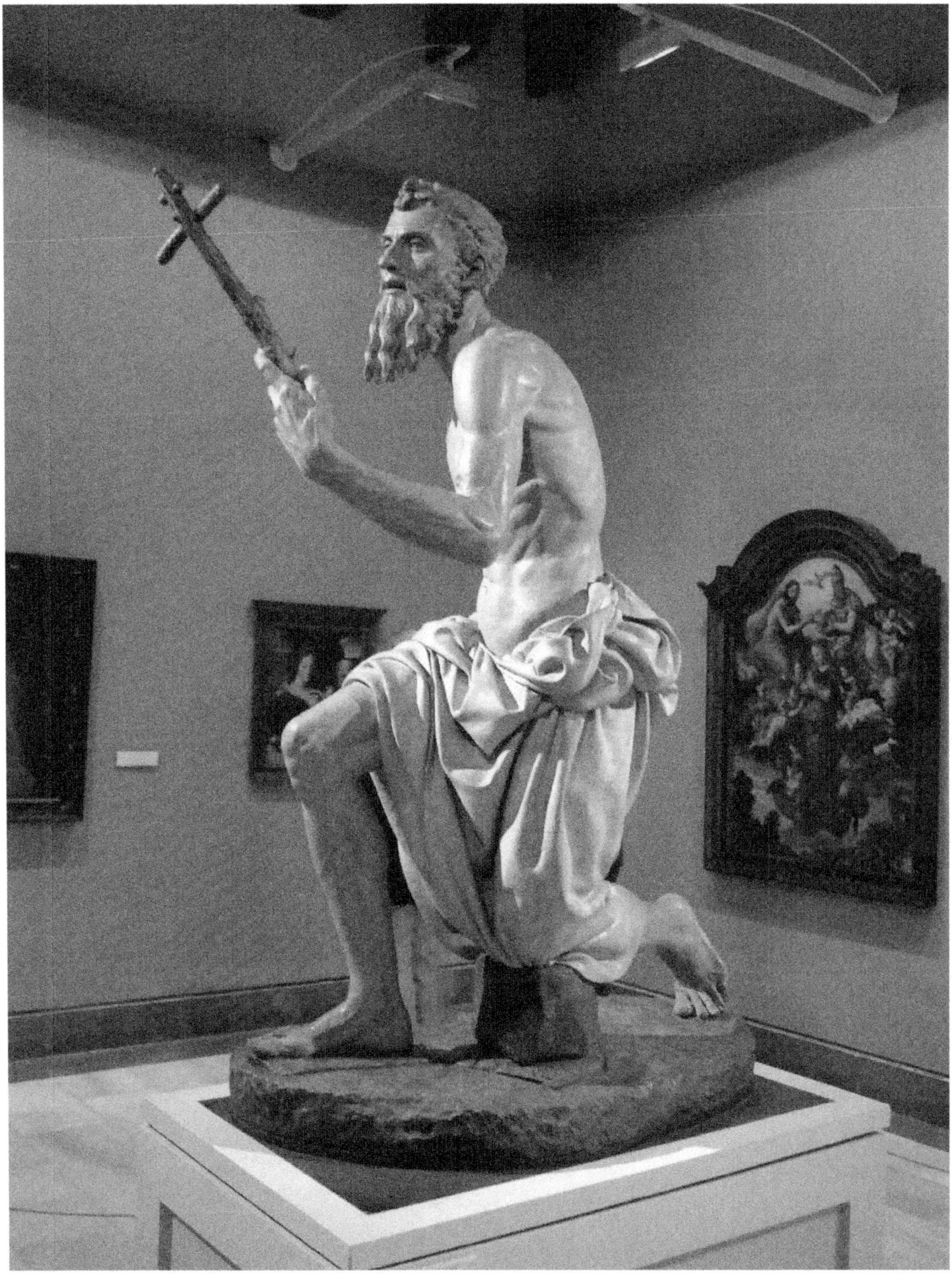

Archaeological Museum

Address: Plaza de América, 5
Opening days: Temporarily closed
Visit times: September to June 9am - 9pm except for Sundays 9am – 3pm
July & August 9am – 3pm
Ticket price: €1.50 (Free for EU citizens)
Audioguide: Not available
Estimated time: 1 – 1.5 hours
Best time: Anytime

The Archaeological Museum of Seville hosts artifacts and art pieces found in the province of Seville from pre-historic times to the Middle Ages, with some Gothic works.

The museum occupies the building of the Fine Arts Pavilion on Ibero-American Expo 1929, designed by Aníbal González and built in a neo-Renaissance style. The museum started a complete renovation of the building in January 2020

The collection includes works of ancient cultures, mainly Roman with a wide group of mosaics and classic sculptures of gods and emperors from different settlements in Seville province. This museum also hosts the *El Carambolo* treasure, consisting of bracelets, necklaces and other accessories made of pure gold.

Tips & Info

The Archaelogical Museum is temporarily closed since January 2019 due to a necessary renovation that will take years. The finest pieces of the museum are originally from Italica, the Roman city 11 kilometres from Seville, which was an important trade centre during the 2nd & 3rd centuries. Two Roman emperors of this time were born in Italica, Trajan and Hadrian, and at the museum you can look at their busts and sculptures.

The museum has a total of 27 exhibit rooms and going around them all can be a bit overwhelming. There is no audio guide available and the descriptive panels can be confusing and difficult to follow. I would recommend that you walk around as you feel, trying not to miss the Diana and Venus representations in marble and the mosaic of Baco.

The most impressive room is the only one open on the first floor, the one guarding the Treasure of Carambolo. The treasure was dated to the 8th century BC as part of the Tartessos culture, but some experts do not agree with this, placing it as part of the Phoenician culture, doubting the existence of Tartessos. This is probably the biggest enigma of our ancient history.

Museum of Arts and Popular Customs

Address: Plaza de América, 3
Opening days: Tuesday to Sunday (Check public holidays)
Visit times: September to June 9am - 9pm except for Sundays 9am – 3pm
July & August 9am – 3pm
Ticket price: €1.50 (Free for EU citizens)
Audioguide: Not available
Estimated time: 1 – 1.5 hours
Best time: Anytime

Ethnology and anthropology are fascinating aspects when we really want to know everything about the area we are visiting. The Museum of Arts and Popular Customs was established with the purpose of spreading local traditions. This is a very interesting approach to the culture of Seville and Andalusia through the centuries, from the cities to the countryside and going through different social classes.

The museum opened its doors in 1973 at the former Mudéjar Pavilion of the Ibero-American Expo and just across from the archaeological museum. At the beginning, it hosted works coming from other museums and private collections. Most of the objects, tools, photographs and clothes displayed now at the museum arrived there after donations made by Andalusian companies or families.

Tips & Info

Most of the visitors coming to Seville will come to Plaza de América to enjoy the beauty of the park and the lovely building of the 1929 Expo, but only a few will decide to visit the interior of the Museum of Arts and Popular Customs.

If you decide to enter you will enjoy this special journey through Andalusian culture. You will have the exhibit rooms distributed in two floors, starting with the basement. These rooms are dedicated to domestic furniture and utensils, artisanal jobs and manufacturing and historical weapons. The ground floor rooms are distributed around the central courtyard. There, you can see a recreation of the Díaz Velázquez family dwelling and their working areas. This family donated all these belongings to the museum in 1979. Other parts of the museum have been chosen to show other aspects of the culture such as music and religion.

The style of the building is neo-Mudéjar, an interpretation of the combination of Moorish and Christian styles very popular in the area during the late middle ages, designed by architect Aníbal González.

After you visit the museum you can go for a walk around Plaza de América, also known by locals as the Square of Doves. Children and adults are often found feeding the birds with seeds you can buy directly there.

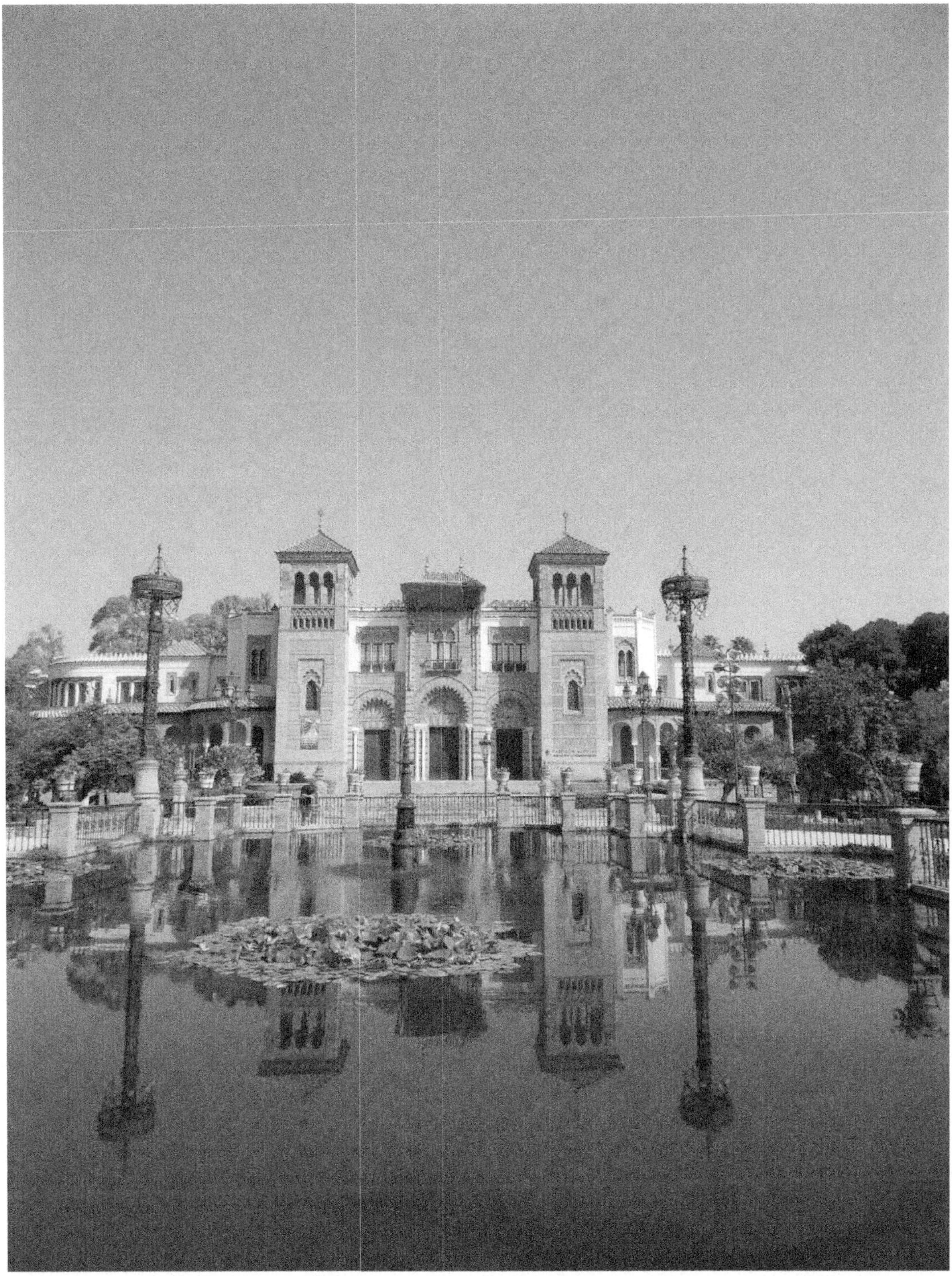

Torre del Oro

Address: Paseo de Critóbal Colón
Opening days: Monday to Sunday (Closed public holidays)
Visit times: Mon to Fri 9.30am -6.45 pm
Weekends 10.30am – 6.45pm
Ticket price: €3 (Concessions €1.50)
Audioguide: Available (€2)
Estimated time: 1 hour
Best time: Anytime

Torre del Oro (Tower of Gold) is a watchtower built along the river side in 1220 and is considered the last Moorish building in the city. The tower was not part of the city walls, but was only linked to them through a single stretch of wall. The purpose of the tower was to defend the access to the city from the river from the Christian troops of the kingdom of Castile, who wished to take back the city.

The name of the tower is linked to its origins and the materials used in its construction: lime, mortar and hay. These materials gave the tower a golden colour that reflected on the river too.

The tower is now home to the Navy Museum of Seville, where the history of the tower is explained. In addition, the museum includes engravings, ships' replicas and artifacts of different historical periods of the Spanish Navy.

Tips & Info

The view of Torre del Oro and the river is recognizable straight away when you get to Seville. Even if you are not interested in the Navy Museum, every visitor should come and at least see the tower.

If you decide to visit the museum, you can rent the audio guide for €2. Do not miss the top floor and the amazing views of the river and the rest of the city from the terrace.

The tower played an important role during the Christian conquest of Seville in 1248. Blocking the river access was a priority for Muslim citizens of the city, who designed the tower as an anchor point that would block the river with a large chain. Across the river another structure would work as the other anchor point. A fleet from Cantabria, a northern Spanish region, broke the chains, leading the Castilians to the conquest. As a consequence, the city surrendered on the 23rd November 1248. This achievement was remembered through the centuries and it is still present in the flag of the autonomous region of Cantabria.

Going back to the name of the tower, there are some theories referring to the storage of gold coming from America during the 16th and 17th century, but that is difficult to believe due to the Arabic language origin of the name of the tower itself, translated later to Spanish.

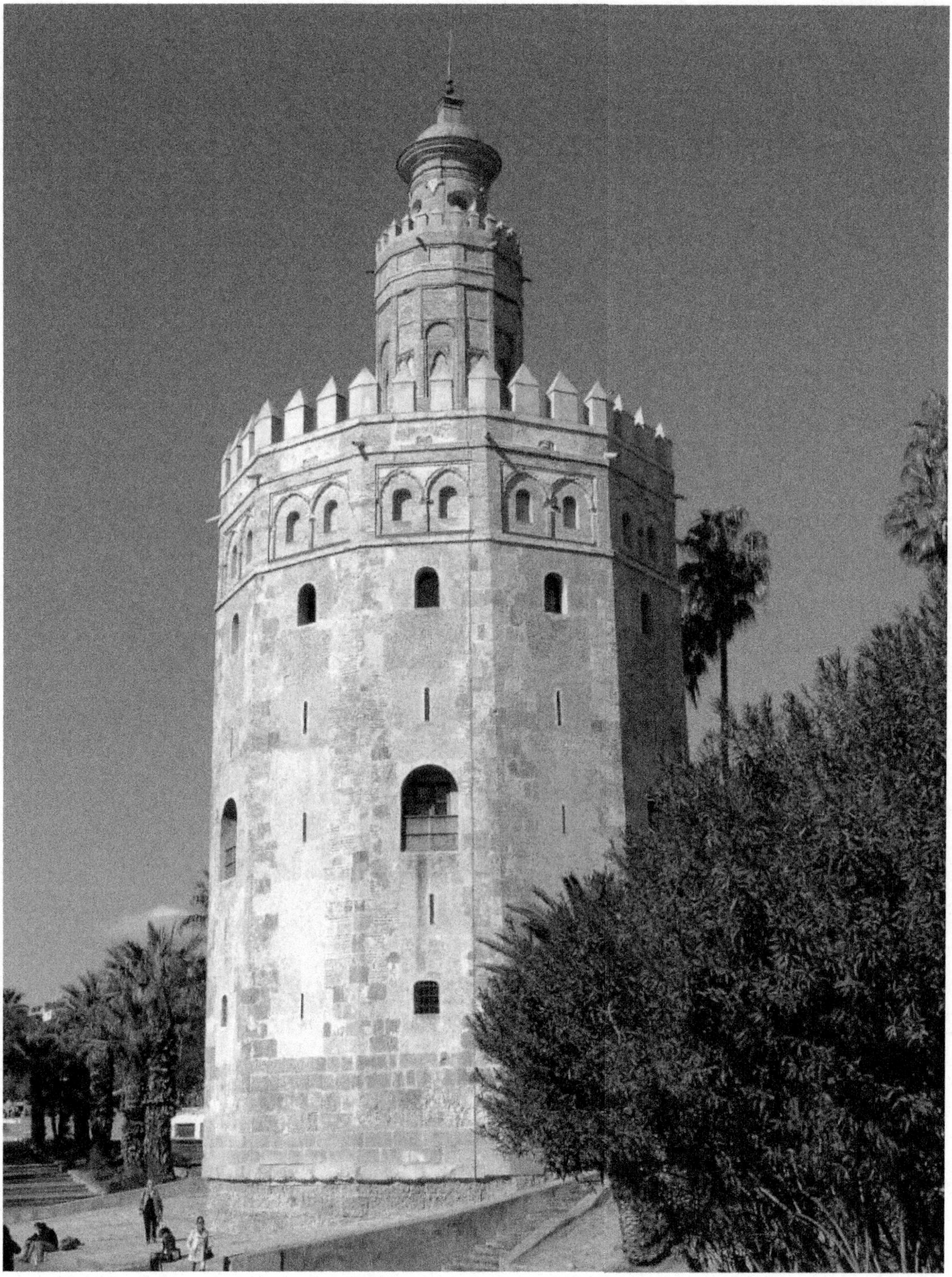

Tobacco Factory

Address: Calle San Fernando, 4
Opening days: Monday to Saturday
Visit times: 8am – 9pm
Ticket price: Free access
Audioguide: Not available
Estimated time: 30 minutes
Best time: Afternoon

The building of the Royal Tobacco Factory of Seville is considered a masterpiece of the industrial architecture of the 1700s. It worked as a factory until 1945, when the cigarette company moved to more modern facilities. In the 1950s, this building passed into the hands of the University of Seville, and is still used as an administration building and the seat for Humanities faculties.

The tobacco industry in Seville has ancient origins. With the arrival of Spaniards to America and the foundation of Casa de la Contratación, Seville became the trade centre for all the products coming from the New World, tobacco being one of the most requested, and the new plant started to manufacture cigarettes in 1757. It was the second largest building in the whole of Spain at its time, only after the Monastery of El Escorial, near Madrid.

Tips & Info

The building of the former Tobacco Factory is located just a few minutes away from the monumental area of the city, in between the cathedral and Plaza de España. Although it is now working as a university building, it is open for visitors. You will be able to explore both courtyards and the Baroque influenced main façade, but nothing more, so as to not interfere in the students' everyday routine. As you enter you will see the magnificent staircase that brings students and academic figures to the upper floor.

It is very curious to see the signs in the interior of the building that still recall its previous use, such as the signs of storerooms, lifts or manufacturing areas. For almost two centuries, hundreds of employees have worked inside those walls. The tobacco factory served as the inspiration for Prosper Merimée, writer of the novel *Carmen*, brought to the opera by the composer Georges Bizet. Carmen, the main character, was a young gipsy lady who used to work at this tobacco factory rolling cigarettes and fell in love with a famous bullfighter called Escamillo. As you can see these and other characters represent the stereotypes of the society of Seville in the mid-1800s.

The women's section of the Royal Tobacco factory was also painted by Gonzalo Bilbao in 1915 and can be seen at the Fine Arts Museum.

Alfonso XIII Hotel

Address: Calle San Fernando, 2
Opening days: Every day
Visit times: 7am – midnight
Ticket price: Free access
Audioguide: Not needed
Estimated time: 30 minutes
Best time: Afternoon coffee

Hotel Alfonso XIII is another masterpiece of early 20th century architecture. It was built for the Ibero-American Expo by architect José Espiau y Muñoz and it was officially opened in April 1928. The building has details of neo-Mudéjar and Andalusian regionalism. The materials, bricks, wood, plaster and ceramic are very common in the area. The hotel was designed as a traditional noble house, with a central courtyard surrounded by different celebration rooms on the ground floor and private areas above them.

The hotel gets its name from the king reigning during that period. Alfonso decided aspects of the building and how the different rooms needed to be disposed too. Alfonso XIII hotel, with a 5-star great luxury category, is a very exclusive accommodation option in Seville. Depending on the season, the royal suite can cost up to €3,500 for one night, but the starting price for an average room will be around €500.

Tips & Info

Hotel Alfonso XIII is a treasure of our architecture and one of the buildings remaining with the same use from Expo 1929. Walking around the common areas is a pleasure and every visitor can immerse themselves in all the details. Once you get into the lobby, you can feel the luxury. Rooms are covered with the finest ceramic tile work, decorated with tapestries and ostentatious lamps. Special mention to the carving work in the wood of the lift doors; do not miss the chance to enjoy it.

Once you have passed the reception desk and shops, leaving the lifts on your right, you will arrive at the central courtyard where the café is. Staying at this hotel is obviously not affordable for every visitor, but there is a low cost option to enjoy the hotel: have a drink in the café. Prices would also be much more expensive than the average of the city, but it is never bad to indulge ourselves from time to time.

The hotel also has three restaurants inside with a wide variety of local dishes and other exotic options. If you want to try any of them, my recommendation would be going to the rooftop, so that apart from a delicious meal, you will enjoy nice views of the city too.

This hotel has hosted celebrities from all over the world, from royalty to Hollywood stars. This hotel has also been used as a set for the successful series, The Crown.

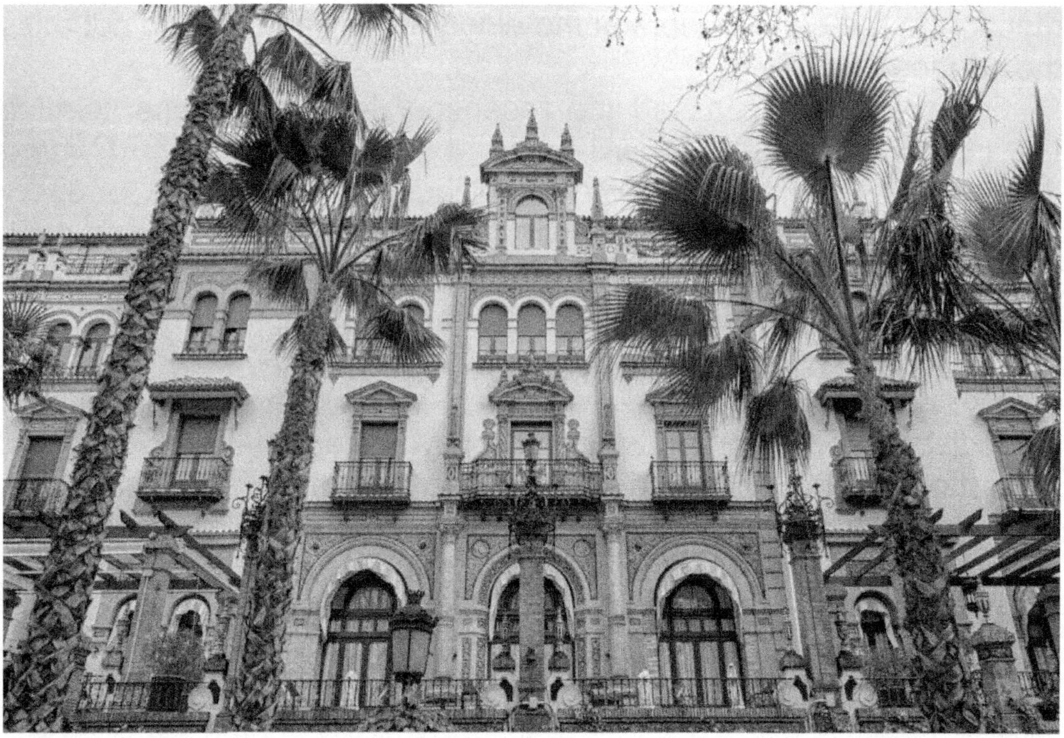

Maria Luisa Park

Address: Paseo de las Delicias
Opening days: Every day
Visit times: 8am – 10pm
Ticket price: Free access
Audioguide: Not available
Estimated time: 1 – 1.5 hours
Best time: Anytime

Maria Luisa Park is a historical garden converted into Seville's principal green area. In 1850, Princess Maria Luisa and her husband the Duke of Montpensier moved to San Telmo Palace, nowadays residence of the Presidency of the Autonomous Government of Andalusia. They bought farming lands around the palace along the river with the intention of creating a massive private garden, designed by the French gardener André Lecotant.

In 1893, Maria Luisa donated to the city part of these gardens, becoming the first urban park in the city. Seville was going to host an Ibero-American Expo in 1929 and from 1910 the gardens were transformed to be part of this big event. Some pavilions were built around and inside the park, like Plaza de España and the museums of Plaza de América. The park we visit nowadays is almost the same that hosted thousands of visitors during the Expo.

Tips & Info

The easiest access to Maria Luisa Park is from Plaza de España. The park has a 340,000sq metres area, so it is good to choose what to visit before you start walking around. You will see at the entrance some maps that can help you to understand how the different areas are distributed. You cannot miss *Gurugú Mount*, nor *The Birds' Pond*.

Maria Luisa Park contains a wide variety of botanic species. It also works as a botanic garden, with educational panels everywhere to inform visitors about the origin or characteristics of the different plants. Animals are also present in this park. It is very common to see doves, ducks, parakeets and swans.

Every part of the park seems to be dedicated to a different literature movement or writer. There are sculptures and plaques with fragments of novels or poems of some of the most famous characters of Spanish literature. Each little square inside the park will have its meaning.

If you get into the park from Plaza de España, you will see a main road with no vegetation. Around that area you will see stands for bike rentals. If you really want to discover every corner of the park, this can be a great option. Also, if you are travelling in a couple or group, you will be able to rent a tandem or pedal cars for more people.

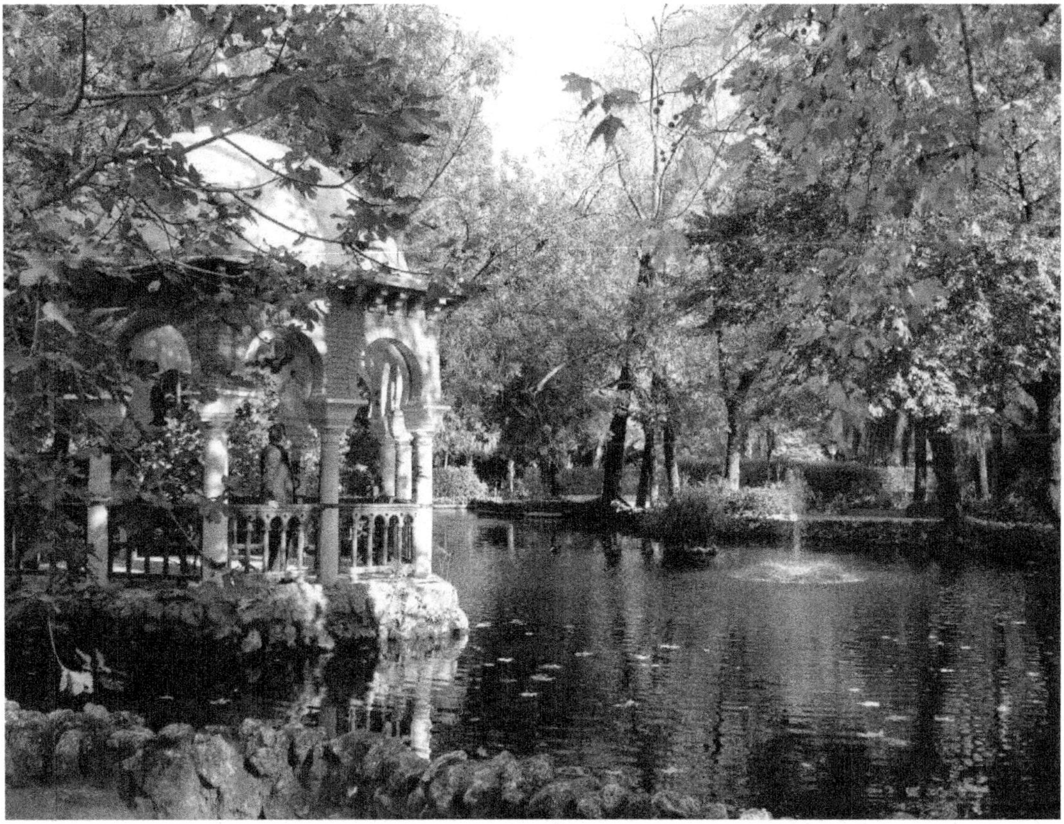

Murillo Gardens

Address: Paseo Catalina de Ribera
Opening days: Every day
Visit times: 7am – midnight
Ticket price: Free access
Audioguide: Not available
Estimated time: 45 minutes
Best time: Anytime

Murillo Gardens is a green area opened along the east defensive walls of the Alcázar and the old city, facing an area of the former Jewish quarter called Santa Cruz. In the 19th century, Seville was starting its industrialization and its walls were an obstacle for the ambitious urban plans of the city council. Avenues were opened around the former walls, creating what we still know as *Ronda Histórica.*

In 1862, the royal family donated the farming lands linked to the Alcazar to the city to host an expansion of the April Fair celebrated nearby. The gardens were opened in 1915 following the design of Juan Talavera.

The gardens now occupy an area of 8,500 sq metres divided into five squares, some of them dedicated to important artists from Seville's past. As the famous Baroque painter Murillo used to live at a house near the gardens, in 1919 the new gardens were named after him.

Tips & Info
You should not miss these gardens if you are passionate about botanics. While not very big, the gardens contain around 50 different species of plants, the most spectacular being the great magnolia trees and the massive ficus macrophylia. These trees and their giant roots catch the eye of every curious visitor. In some parts of the

gardens, like the closest to the Alcazar walls, it is not possible to get close to these trees, but close to Glorieta García Ramos you will be free to walk on the enormous roots of the ficus.

You can get to Murillo Gardens from the Jewish quarter, from Plaza Alfaro or Plaza de Santa Cruz. This last square used to host the church with the same name, where some Murillo paintings were displayed and the one chosen as a resting place for the Baroque artist.

In the long part of the garden, Paseo Catalina de Ribera, a huge monument will catch your attention, consisting of two pillars with a ship across and a lion on top. The monument completed in 1921 is dedicated to Admiral Cristopher Colombus, and very much linked to the city of Seville.

At one side of the garden you will also find a bar where you can rest and have a drink. It is also typical for flamenco dancers and singers to perform in these gardens.

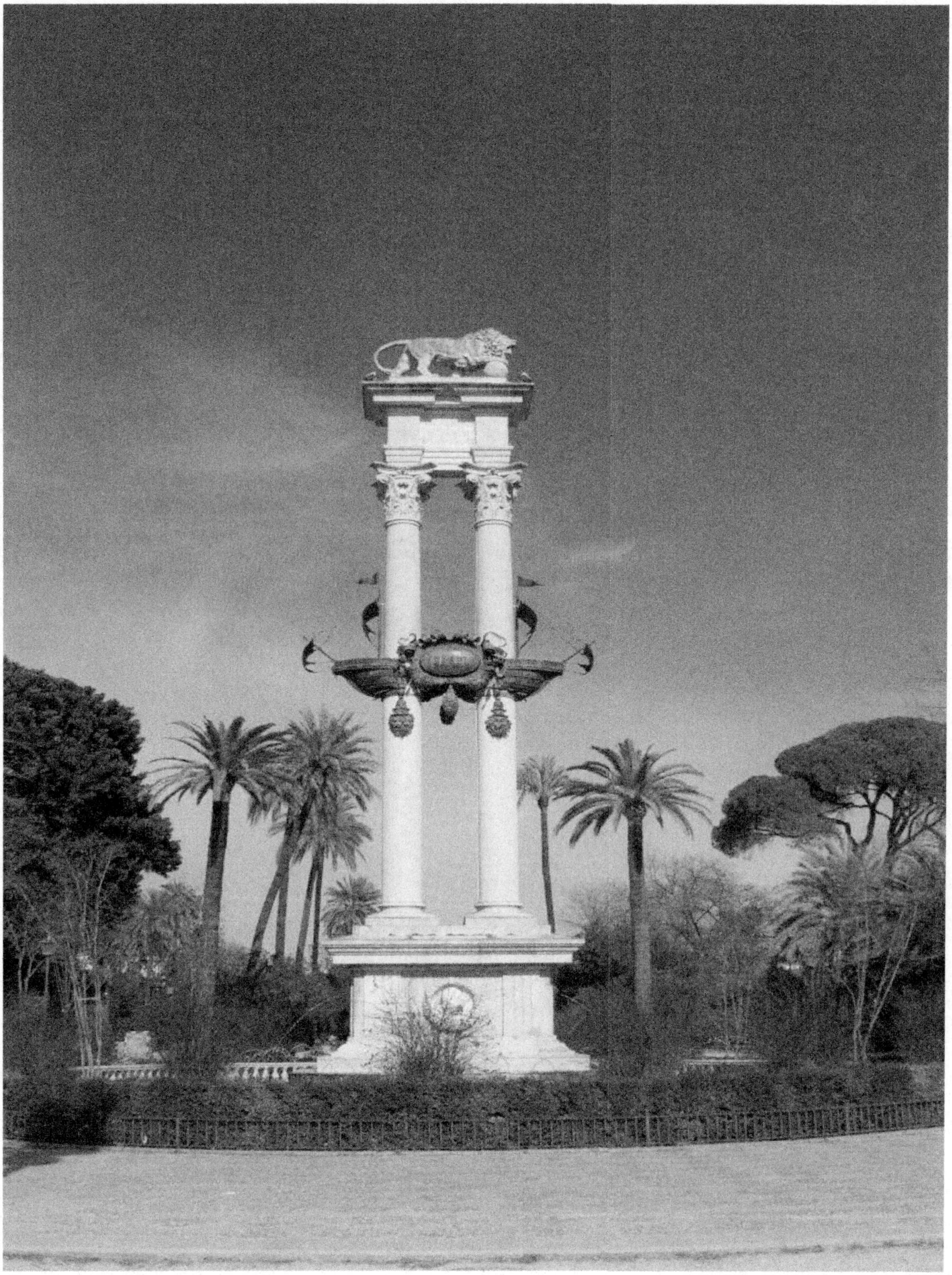

Charity Hospital

Address: Calle Temprado, 3
Opening days: Every day (check public holidays)
Visit times: 10am – 7.30pm
Closed on Sundays 12.30am – 2pm
Ticket price: €8 (Concessions €5)
Audioguide: Included
Estimated time: 1 – 1.5 hours
Best time: Anytime

The Charity Hospital has its origin in the brotherhood with the same name founded in Seville in the middle of the 15th century. The main purpose of the hospital was moving ill people without possibilities to care houses, assisting them spiritually and also burying those who had no resources. The brotherhood completely changed with the entry of Miguel de Mañara as a member, expanding their purpose to include looking after and healing the poor and sick.

The hospital and its church were built in the 1670s in a Baroque style. Some of the best artists of the city took part in these works, such us the great painters Murillo and Valdés Leal or the master sculptor Pedro Roldán. Miguel de Mañara designed the iconography of the church with the clear objective of showing how ephemeral life is and the necessity of work in charity to gain salvation.

Tips & Info

The church of the Charity Hospital is recognised as one of the greatest examples of Baroque in Seville. Miguel de Mañara was a cultured and rich man who invested a lot of money in charitable works after the death of his wife and a period of meditation. The level of literacy in Seville in the 1600s was very low and poverty, famine and misery were present all over the city. The church and its paintings are displayed to be read, as a giant comic, with the seven works of charity as a path to gain the salvation of the soul.

Miguel de Mañara is frequently linked to the legend of Don Juan, a literary character also brought to the opera with the name of Don Giovanni. The final repentance of the character is linked to Mañara, a rich man that dedicated the rest of his life to support helpless people and provide resources to heal their diseases.

It is highly recommended to visit the hospital and church with the audioguide included in the ticket price. When you get to the church you will see the six paintings representing works of charity, but only two of them are original, the other four are only replicas. During the Napoleonic invasions of the 1810s, these paintings were taken by Marshal Soult and brought to France. His heirs decided to sell them and nowadays they are part of the collection of great museums like the Ermitage, in Russia and the British, Canadian and US National Galleries.

Venerables Hospital

Address: Plaza de los Venerables, 8
Opening days: Every day (check public holidays)
Visit times: September to June 10am – 6pm
July & August 10am – 2pm & 5.30pm – 9pm
Ticket price: €10 (Concessions €8)
Audioguide: Included
Estimated time: 1 hour
Best time: Anytime

The Venerables priests' hospital was home to a brotherhood whose duty was to give assistance to those priests who were elderly, helpless and suffering from diseases. It maintained its function until the 1970s as a residence for ecclesiastic members. The hospital and church were built in Baroque style at the end of the 17th century. The central courtyard is a clear example of the style of patios in Seville. The rooms around the courtyard worked as a nursery in past times, while those on the first floor were the private rooms of the residents. The Baroque church is the most picturesque part of the complex, full of frescos by Valdés Leal and his son Lucas Valdés.

The exhibition room is home to some works of Murillo, Pacheco, Montañés and the great master Diego Velázquez.

Tips & Info

The Hospital of Venerables is not easy to find due to its location in between of the extremely narrow streets of the former Jewish quarter. The entrance is facing Plaza de los Venerables, one of the handfuls of open spaces in this whole neighbourhood. Although the outside does not look very impressive, the interior is well worth it.

Once you get to the first patio, you can purchase your ticket and an audio guide will be given to you. You should start by visiting the exhibit room, part of what is called Centro Velázquez. The painting of Saint Rufina is the star work of this exhibit. The next step would be the different courtyards and of course the church. Take your time to visit it and please do not miss the sacristy and its frescos by Valdés Leal, made with the technique of *Trompe l-oeil*. This technique tries to create optical illusion in the visitor, working with the architecture and its dimensions.

If you like ecclesiastical music, you should have a look at the organ, built by the German master Gerharz Grenging in 1991. Organ is not very popular nowadays, but this institution promotes this instrument. You can ask at the ticket office for the organ concerts inside the church of Venerables Hospital, which also hosts a famous international festival.

Divino Salvador Church

Address: Plaza del Salvador, 3
Opening days: Every day (check public holidays). **Please note that this is an active church and this calendar can change**
Visit times: Monday to Saturday 11am – 6pm & Sundays 3pm – 7.30pm
Ticket price: €5 (included with the cathedral)
Audioguide: Included (not with the cathedral ticket)
Estimated time: 45 minutes
Best time: Anytime

The Church of Divino Salvador is the second most important church of the dioceses of Seville after the cathedral. The area occupied by the church was previously the site of Ibn Adabbas Mosque built in the 800s. The same building, after some works, was used as a church once Christians conquered the city in 1248.

Due to the poor restoration works throughout the centuries, in the 1600s, the cathedral council decided to demolish the whole building with the intention of constructing a new church. The new Salvador church, built in Baroque style, was inaugurated in 1712.

Tips & Info

The Church of El Salvador is located in the square with the same name, a few minutes' walk from the cathedral. You can keep the ticket you got at the cathedral and skip the line to get into the church or if you prefer, you can visit Divino Salvador first and skip the line at the cathedral.

It is highly recommended to go around the church with the audio guide so as not to miss any piece of information. The audio device price is €4 if you are entering with the ticket purchased at the cathedral and it is included in the price in case you just visit Divino Salvador.

The church has a rectangular shape, supported by pillars. In its interior you will find a total of 14 chapels and altarpieces. The church is also home for two of the most devoted brotherhoods of Seville's Holy Week, *El Amor* and *Pasión*. The images of these brotherhoods are some of the most venerated by local Catholics and thousands will congregate at the Salvador square to see the processions.

Around the church, in Calle Córdoba, there is a small gate that brings you to the lateral part of the church. There you will find the ablutions courtyard of the former Mosque built in 829. The courtyard is now decorated with orange trees, but it is very curious to see the arches and columns that give us an idea of how the level of the ground has been growing with the passing centuries.

The square of El Salvador is a very typical meeting point for locals to have a chat over a beer and take an appetizer. Do not miss the chance of feeling like a local and take a break in this lovely location.

Saint Louis of France Church

Address: Calle San Luis, 37
Opening days: Tuesday to Sunday
Visit times: 10am – 2pm & 4pm – 8pm
Ticket price: €4 (Concessions €2)
Audioguide: €3
Estimated time: 45 minutes
Best time: Anytime

The Church of Saint Louis is the greatest example of Baroque architecture in Seville in the 18th century. It was built by the Society of Jesus and since Jesuits were expelled from Spain in 1835, it has had different uses. Nowadays it is not a place of worship and it is exclusively opened for the cultural visits after a deep restoration.

The façade is very well decorated with Baroque elements imitating the altar screens of the interior and its spiral columns. The church plan follows the shape of a Greek cross with a central dome. The dome is supported by four pillars that would also separate the four internal chapels around the transept. The altarpieces of the interior are all work of Duque Cornejo from the 1730s. This artist also worked in the Cathedral of Seville, but his masterpiece is the choir of the Mosque-Cathedral in Córdoba.

Tips & Info

This church of Saint Louis was closed for almost 30 years due to the poor state of preservation and only opened its gates to visitors in 2016. This site surprises every visitor before entering. The location in the middle of San Luis Street is not ideal and we know now that a wider square was supposed to be opened in front of the church.

Once inside I would recommend renting the audio guide for €3, or buying the official book for €6.

It is very interesting to see how every corner of the church is amazingly decorated, proof of this late-Baroque style. The altarpieces are full of convex mirror, made of mercury and tin, which create a game of reflections. The light is projected to every part of the church. Beside the church you will find the domestic chapel, part of the former Jesuits' novitiate house linked to the church. This chapel was privately used by the residents.

Santa María La Blanca Church

Address: Calle Santa Maria La Blanca, 5
Opening days: Every day
Visit times: Monday - Saturday 10am - 1pm & 6 pm – 8.30pm. Sundays 9.30am - 12pm & 6pm – 8.30pm
Ticket price: Donation
Audioguide: Not available
Estimated time: 30 minutes
Best time: Anytime

The Church of Santa María La Blanca is one of the most characteristic buildings of Seville city centre. The church was built in Gothic-Mudejar style during the 1400s, while the interior is mainly Baroque.

The church is divided into three naves, the central one higher than the laterals. The ceilings are carefully decorated with plaster work, with only two lateral chapels, one for baptisim and the other for sacraments. The church was decorated by some of the best artists of the city during the 1600s. Out of the five works Murillo painted for this church, only the one representing The Last Supper is original, as the rest were taken during the French occupation. In their place, only replicas are displayed nowadays.

Tips & Info

The church of Santa Maria La Blanca is located between the areas of Saint Bartolomé and Santa Cruz, in the middle of the former Jewish quarter. During the 13th century this space was occupied by one of the three synagogues of the city. The synagogue was taken after the rebellion against the Jews of 1391 and a church was built instead.

According to the sources and excavations, this building would have an older origin. At both sides of the entrance, you can distinguish two pillars, one of which has an inscription in Latin. Also going to the side entrance in Calle Archeros, you can see two columns with Visigoth *chapiters*.

The visit to the church is free of charge, but as you enter, you will see an urn where visitors make donations for the cultural visit. Unfortunately there is neither audio guide nor any other source of information, so it is recommended to get some from the internet if you want to deeply understand every corner of this magnificent church. Please note that as an active church, there could be religious services being held inside.

On the left side of the façade you will see the plaque of Sefarad, the sign remembering the Medieval Jewish areas in Spanish cities.

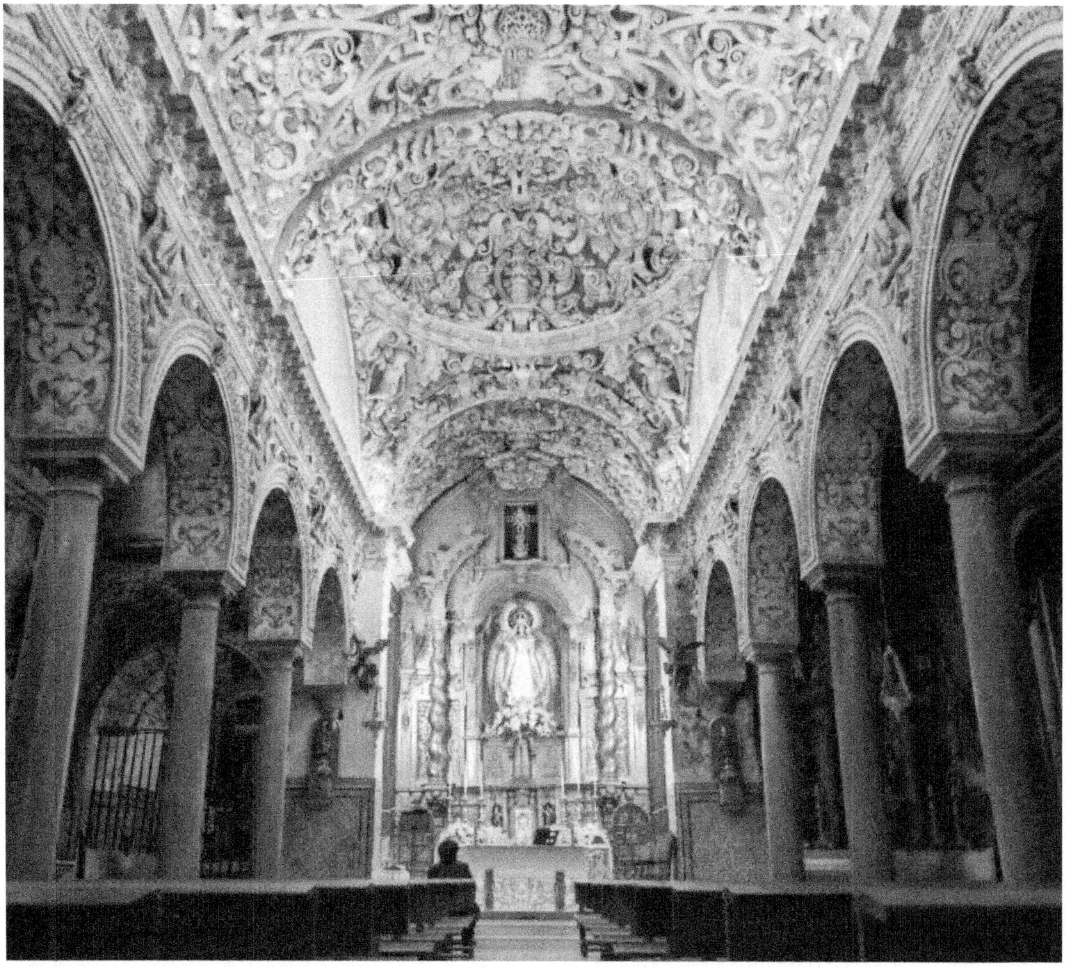

Triana

Opening days: Every day
Ticket price: Free
Audioguide: Not needed
Estimated time: 2 hours
Best time: Anytime

Triana is the name given to the district across the Guadalquivir River. It is considered the first suburb of the city and one of the most authentic areas to walk around. It has traditionally been separated from the city by the river and throughout the centuries that has created a special atmosphere.

It probably has Roman origins as a fixed settlement, even if we have older remains in the area. Triana is also considered the birthplace of flamenco in Seville due to the gipsy population. Since the 12th century, this area was linked to the city by a floating bridge made of boats that disappeared in the mid-1800s. In its place, we can see the Triana Bridge. The remains of Saint George's castle are still visible by the river shore. This structure was the only defensive building of the neighbourhood and became important for the defense of the city.

The main church of Triana is called *Santa Ana,* popularly called by locals the Cathedral of Triana.

Tips & Info

Triana is a lovely area to walk around and spend half a day of your stay in Seville. You can get to the area by crossing Isabel II Bridge to get to Plaza del Altozano. At that square you can find Triana Market, where you can try some of the most typical products. The remains of Saint George's castle can be found at the end of this market. Apart from a defensive structure, this castle was also the site for the inquisition in Seville.

You can continue your walk along the river by Betis Street, called after the Roman name of this river and enjoy the view of the city centre. In Betis Street there are some places where flamenco is performed and that could be a good place to rest and enjoy a live show.

You cannot leave Triana without getting into Santa Ana Church. This is considered the first church built in Seville after the Christian conquest of 1248. Its style is Gothic-Mudéjar and its exterior seems to be closer to a defensive structure than to religious. The reason is that Triana was never surrounded by walls and every public building needed to be ready for an enemy attack. The church is also linked to holy week as it originally was the destination point of all the processions of the Triana district. Nowadays, all the brotherhoods of Triana will cross the river and go to the cathedral.

Jewish Quarter

Opening days: Every day
Ticket price: Free
Audioguide: Not needed
Estimated time: 1 – 1.5 hours
Best time: Anytime

The Jewish quarter of Seville is the area nowadays occupied by the neighbourhoods of Santa Cruz and San Bartolomé, near the monumental area.

After the Christian conquest of 1248, this area of the city was offered to the Jewish community who were previously spread throughout Seville during the Muslim rule. This area had four synagogues and very active markets. In 1391 there was a revolt against Jews that had to abandon their worship places. During the following years, the persecutions pushed Jews to convert to Christianity and hide the practice of their own religion. The Jews were expelled in 1492 by Isabella and Ferdinand, known as the Catholic Kings. Jewish people never came back to the area and their presence is only remembered by the names of some of the streets. This area hosts some of the most iconic sites of all Seville city centre, like Plaza de Doña Elvira, Plaza de Santa Cruz and Callejón del Agua.

Tips & Info

The former Jewish Quarter is the area that best preserves the medieval atmosphere of the city. The original urbanism is still present with some renovations, mainly those of the early 20th century.

A walk around this area is mandatory for any visitor to Seville. You can hire a guide to understand better all the history behind those walls. You can walk around the walls of the Alcazar getting to

Callejón del Agua (Water Alley), named after the two pipes preserved inside the defensive walls. Another stop should be at Susona Street, or better said, "Street of death", where you can see a tile remembering an intriguing story that involved a Jewish girl and a Christian man.

You can rest and sit in any of the benches of Doña Elvira square under the shade of orange trees, a hidden spot out of the big crowds. Later you can go to Plaza de Santa Cruz, where one of the synagogues used to be. This synagogue was replaced by a Gothic church that was demolished during the French invasion of 1810. I would highly recommend going to Calle Verde (green street), a narrow alley off the beaten path covered with green vines. Some of the houses belong to a hotel that still preserves medieval tunnels of Jewish times.

As you walk, you will notice signs with the inscription *Caminos de Sefarad*, as in every former Jewish quarter around Spain. Sefarad was the name given by Jews to the Iberian Peninsula. This area is also famous for its gastronomy. Do not miss the opportunity of trying local tapas in any of the bars, but be aware that the Santa Cruz area is very popular for tourists and you should look for recommendations.

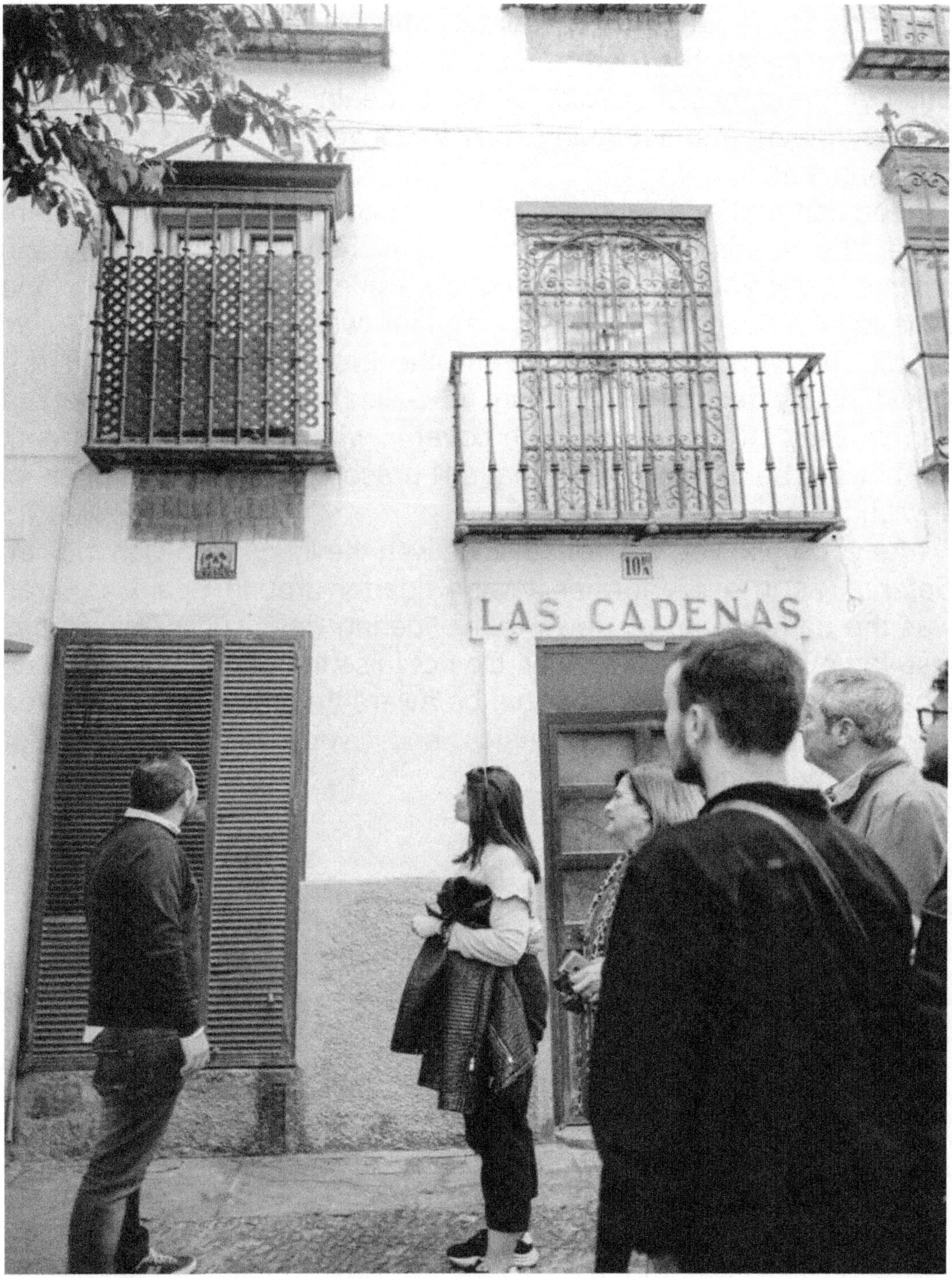
10
LAS CADENAS

Alameda & Macarena

Opening days: Every day
Ticket price: Free
Audioguide: Not needed
Estimated time: 1 – 1.5 hours
Best time: Anytime

Alameda and Macarena would have been the areas of the north side of the old city of Seville. Alameda de Hércules is the name of a big square surrounded by bars where many locals would gather. The square is full of white poplar trees, *álamo* in Spanish. It opened in 1574 and it is considered the oldest public garden in Europe. In ancient times, the Guadalquivir River crossed this area and the floods were frequent until the course of the river was changed.

The whole area gets the name of Macarena after the northern gate of the city, the only one still standing along with the defensive walls built by the Moors in the 11th and 12th centuries. Most of the city walls were demolished during the 19th century, preserving only this stretch of walls together with those of the Alcázar.

Macarena is also the name of one of the most beloved devotions of the Virgin in Seville and the basilica is another highlight of the area.

Tips & Info

The north area of the city centre is probably the one least known by tourists. Most of the visitors will stay around the monumental area and will not know even about the existence of this wonderful area.

Alameda gets its name from Hercules, founder of the city according to mythology. Both sides of the oval square have four pillars, with sculptures of Hercules and Julius Caesar on the south side and two lions with the shields of Seville and Spain on the north.

The south columns were brought to Alameda from a Roman temple dated in the 2nd century located in Calle Mármoles.

If you want to feel like a local you should go to the Basilica of Macarena. Apart from the church you can visit the museum attached dedicated to the brotherhood. It is a very interesting way to learn about the Holy Week. The silver and gold works, standards and even the floats are displayed at the museum. The entrance fee is €5.

The square of Alameda is also very trendy for locals that go out for a drink or looking for something to eat. You will have as many options as you want, from traditional meals to tapas or modern cuisine and the same with pubs and night clubs. Every style is welcomed.

GASTRONOMICAL SEVILLE

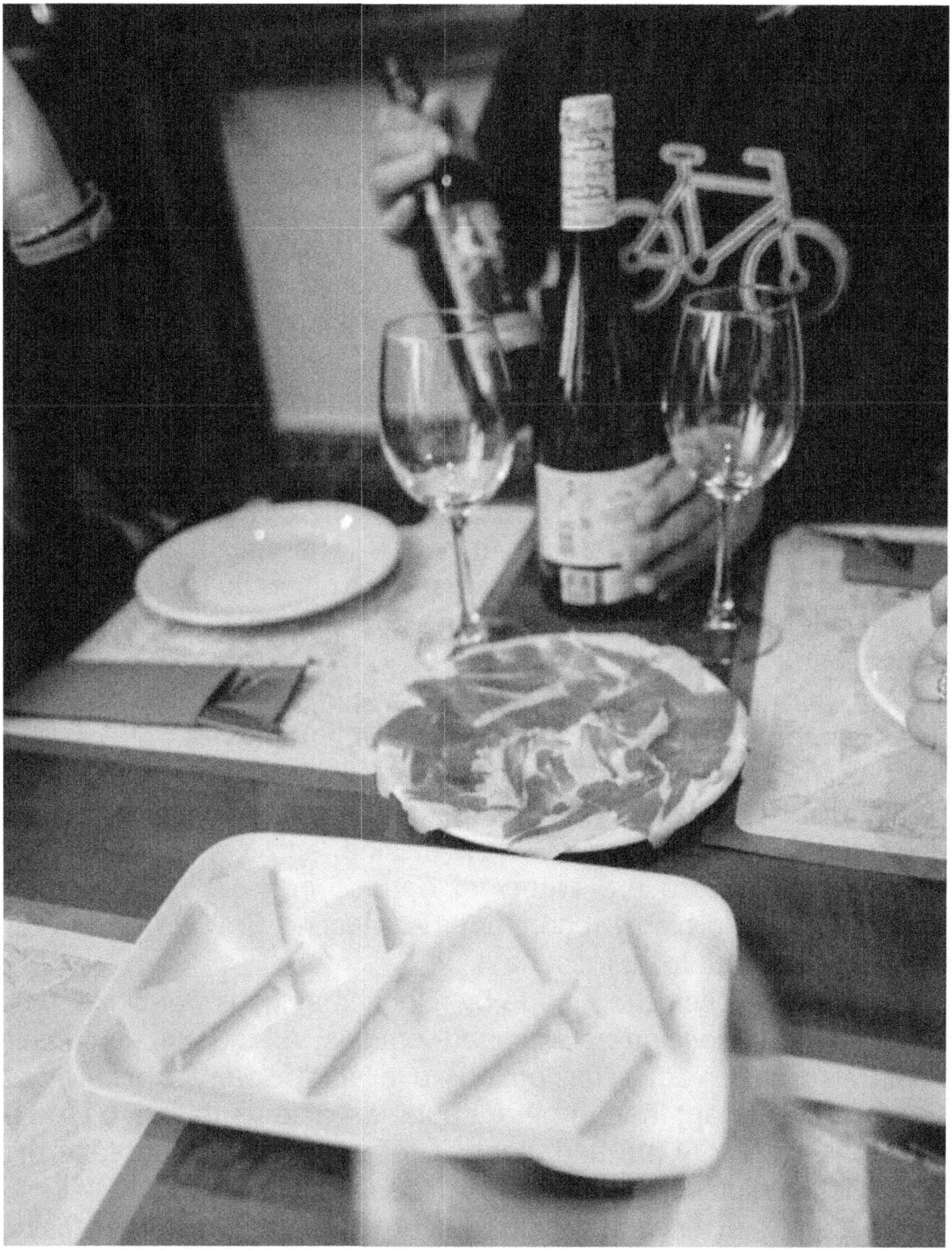

Seville is the capital city of the southern Spanish region of Andalusia. With a rich history and impressive monuments, Seville has become a very attractive destination for travellers. Not everything is about touring monuments though, as the Andalusian cuisine is also a highlight of any trip.

Lots of different civilisations have left their culinary stamp on this region. Seville is a city with a warm climate, where locals go out on a regular basis to share moments with relatives and friends over a nice meal or simply over a beer or glass of wine.

All restaurants and bars included in this book are well known by locals and some of them have hosted several generations of Sevillians. Each of them is special because of a different aspect; not only the quality of the meal served, but also their atmosphere, history or interior design. The average quality of the food served in the different bars and restaurants in Seville is very high, while the prices are very reasonable too. The service given by restaurant staff is generally very good. You will feel welcome in any bar or restaurant you choose.

With the arrival of tourism, many new places have opened their doors around the city centre, offering a wide variety of options. The amount of competitors have also made restaurant owners innovate in their dishes, focusing in some cases on fusion cuisine. If you are interested in learning about local cuisine and want to join any cooking class, there are plenty of options in the different online platforms. I would highly recommend contacting *Sevilla Food* for an amazing class held by a local host.

This is only a selection made by a local that loves traditional food as well as experiencing new culinary options. All the places chosen would also have vegetarian options available. Spanish meal times are usually different than in other countries. The usual lunch time is between 2pm and 4 pm and dinner after 9pm. You should take this into consideration when looking for places to eat in Seville.

I will explain the reason why every restaurant has been listed here, and some information and recommendations about the different places like the area, or what to order. All these restaurants have the great advantage of being located in a producer region where the quality of products themselves is unrivalled, from the coasts of the Mediterranean to the agriculture fields of the interior and livestock in the mountain area. Seville has a lot to offer and I would like you to enjoy it to the maximum.

¡BUEN PROVECHO!

Tapas Bars and Traditional Cuisine

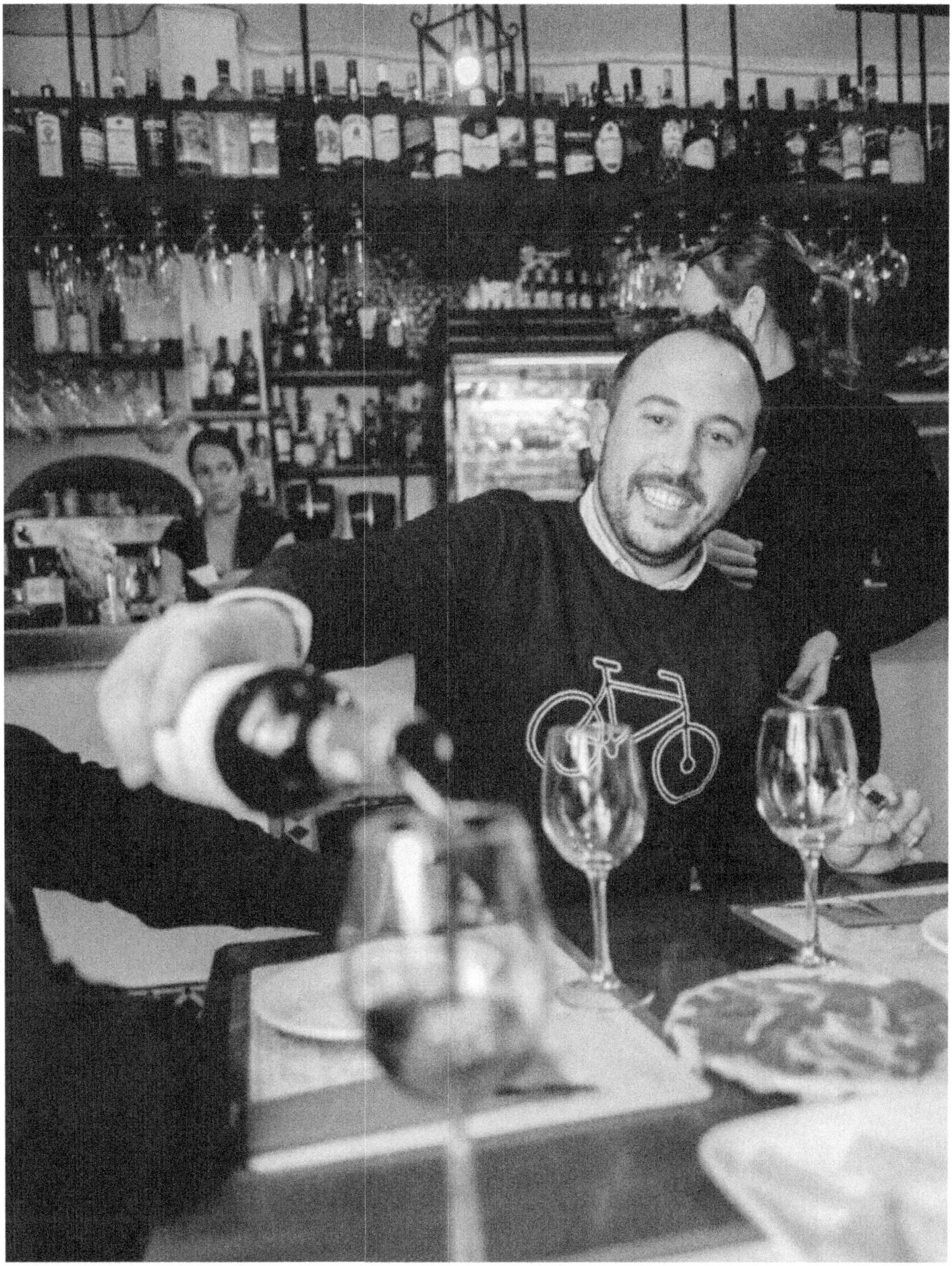

El Rincón de Murillo

Address: Calle Lope de Rueda, 18
Area: Santa Cruz
Opening day: Every day
Opening times: 8am – 1 am
Type: Tapas & Restaurant
What to order: Pork Cheeks

This traditional tapas bar and restaurant is located at a little corner of the former Jewish quarter, beside one of the narrowest streets in the whole city (Calle Reinoso).

At the end of this street you will see the outside tables of this tapas bar and restaurant. You can stay outside or ask for a table inside, depending on the weather. Even if you stay outside, go and have a look at the interior. You will be surprised by the glass floor that allows you to see an old underground wine cellar.

The food served at this restaurant is mainly traditional, with lots of fried fish and meat stews. Spanish cuisine is all about pork. The culture of pork in Andalusia refers to historical reasons (forbidden animal for Muslims and Jewish) and it is still commonly served everywhere. I have chosen the pork cheeks as their star dish due to its tenderness and flavour, you will not be disappointed.

Casa Ricardo – Antigua Casa Ovidio

Address: Calle Hernán Cortés, 2
Area: San Lorenzo
Opening days: Tuesday to Sunday
Opening times: 1pm – 4.30pm & 8pm – midnight (except Sundays)
Type: Tapas & Restaurant
What to order: Croquettes

This place has been open since 1898 with different names depending on the owners, Ricardo being the last one. It has always preserved its authentic atmosphere, decorated with pictures of the sculptures carried during Holy Week processions. It is located at a quiet street in the San Lorenzo neighbourhood, but people from all over the city come here to try the amazing croquettes, which are cooked to perfection. Croquettes are made with béchamel and ham, which are covered in breadcrumbs and then deep-fried. We do not know what the secret of the croquettes of Casa Ricardo is, but the truth is that the béchamel is much more liquid than the usual version and creates a different texture. During Lent, due to the religious restriction of eating meat, they would serve cod croquettes instead of ham.

Blanco Cerrillo

Address: Calle José de Velilla, 1
Area: Duque / Campana
Opening days: Monday to Saturday
Opening times: 7.30am – 11.30pm
Type: Tapas / Beer
What to order: Adobo

Blanco Cerrillo seems to be a very old fashioned bar, but is one of those places every local knows about in Seville. You would not need to go inside to understand why this place is special. The smell of the whole street gives you the answer: *adobo.*

In a region surrounded by both the Mediterranean and the Atlantic, fish should be an important part of the culture. In Andalusia, you can try a wide variety of fish. *Boquerones en Adobo* is the star dish here, "boquerones" being the name of the fish (anchovies) while "en adobo" refers to the cooking method (marinated). Anchovies will be marinated in a sauce with vinegar, paprika, garlic and oregano for few hours before deep-frying. You do not need to stay at this place for long. Try to get a small spot at the bar or stand in one of the few tables outside, order a beer and a tapa and keep exploring the city.

En la Espero te Esquina

Address: Calle Corral del Rey, 10
Area: Alfalfa
Opening days: Tuesday to Sunday
Opening times: 9am – 4.30pm
8pm – midnight (except Sundays)
Type: Tapas
What to order: Mantecado al whisky

The first thing to know about this place is that it does not have floor staff and you should order at the bar. Then you can sit at any table and you will be called when you meal is ready. This bar has very reasonable prices with tapas about €3 and it is commonly frequented by locals.

The name of the place has no literal translation, but a word game with no actual meaning. Some of the tapas served here are *montaditos* or *pepitos*, small sandwiches filled with Iberian meats or cheese. The tapa I have chosen is called *Mantecado al whisky*, and it is one of these sandwiches. It has a pork loin fillet with a sauce with garlic, lemon and a reduction of white wine and whisky. En la Espero te Esquina is one of those bars you can find at any neighbourhood, but in this case is located in the very centre of the city.

Bodeguita Antonio Romero

Address: Calle Antonio Díaz, 19
Area: Arenal
Opening days: Tuesday to Sunday
Opening times: 12pm – midnight
Type: Tapas / Restaurant
What to order: Piripi

Antonio Romero is one of the classics of Andalusian cuisine in Seville city centre. After opening the first bar in 1994, nowadays they have four spots in the same area, some more focused on tapas and others actual restaurants.

For this spot, I have chosen a tapa and you should know that tapas can only be ordered at the bar or at a high table. If you decide to have a seat, you would have to order medium or full portions to share. The *piripi* is a small sandwich called *montadito* and filled with cheese, bacon, natural tomato and pork loin. It looks kind of heavy and it actually is, so please be careful when ordering not to waste food.

Fish is also delicious at Antonio Romero, mainly fried in Andalusian style, like squid, cod or dogfish, small shark cut into small pieces and marinated.

Pepe Hillo

Address: Calle Adriano, 24
Area: Arenal
Opening days: Tuesday to Sunday
Opening times: 12pm – midnight
Type: Tapas / Restaurant
What to order: Cola de toro (Oxtail)

Pepe Hillo is located in the Arenal neighbourhood just opposite one of the gates of the bullring. This has been traditionally known as the bullfighters' area and this restaurant preserves part of that history.

The place is divided into two zones, bar and restaurant. Tapas can only be ordered at the bar, but if you prefer a more formal lunch or dinner you can always go to the big room and ask for a table. The bar is usually packed, so please do not stress and enjoy. Make sure you have a small piece of bar or a high table before ordering. This is a self-service bar and you will be called when your meal is ready.

The decor is dedicated to bullfighting with some mounted bull heads displayed on the walls. Being in such a place, the star dish has to be the oxtail, slow cooked and stewed, simply tasty.

El Pasaje

Address: Pasaje de Vila, 8
Area: Santa Cruz
Opening days: Every day
Opening times: 12.30pm – midnight
Type: Tapas
What to order: Torta de Inés Rosales

You can find El Pasaje while walking around the streets of Santa Cruz, the former Jewish quarter. It is located at a corner with only high tables outside and a few regular tables in its interior.

The cuisine here brings some innovation to the traditional Andalusian meals. The dish chosen is *torta de Inés Rosales* and it consists of a crispy sweet pastry topped with chicken curry and sweet chilli sauce. This pastry with olive oil is a typical sweet from the area commercialised by Inés Rosales and commonly sold as souvenirs from Seville.

Apart from being a tapas bar, El Pasaje is also popular among locals and visitors to have a drink. The kitchen will close at midnight every day, but on Fridays and Saturdays the bar will be open serving beer and cocktails until 3am.

Bodega Santa Cruz (Las Columnas)

Address: Calle Rodrigo Caro, 1
Area: Santa Cruz
Opening days: Every day
Opening times: 11.30am – midnight
Type: Tapas
What to order: Montadito de pringá

Although the official name of the bar is Bodega Santa Cruz referring to the area where it is located, everybody in Seville will know this place as Las Columnas. The porch of the entrance is supported by two big pillars.

There is no floor staff, so you should find a comfortable spot at the bar or any of the small tables before ordering. You will see that many people around you are only drinking and the reason is that lots of locals love going to Las Columnas just to drink. The food is good and traditional too and out of the big menu displayed on the walls you should go for *Montadito de pringá*. Pringá is the name of the combination of meats usually served with broth, in this case all mixed up and filling a small sandwich. Another interesting detail about this place is that the waiter will write down your bill with chalk on the bar. Be careful and do not delete it!

Las Golondrinas

Address: Calle Pagés del Corro, 76
Area: Triana
Opening days: Tuesday to Sunday
Opening times: 12pm – 4.30pm
8pm – midnight
Type: Tapas / Restaurant
What to order: Mushrooms

Triana is a wonderful area of the city and so is its cuisine. In one of the main streets of the neighbourhood you will find Las Golondrinas, a very characteristic bar for locals. It is divided into two parts; tapas are only served at the bar but you can sit on the first floor and order half and full portions to share.

The reason this place is listed in this book is without any doubt the mushroom recipe. Mushrooms are served grilled with a creamy green sauce. It is a must try when you go to Triana, even if you stop at the bar for just a drink and one tapa of mushrooms.

You will see there are two bars with the same name in Triana. The original, located in Calle Antillano Campos, is smaller and a bit old fashioned, but the menu is similar and of course you will have mushrooms served there too.

Blanca Paloma

Address: Calle San Jacinto, 49
Area: Triana
Opening days: Monday to Saturday
Opening times: 12.30pm – 4.30pm
8.30pm – midnight (except Monday)
Type: Tapas / Restaurant
What to order: Albóndigas de chocos (Squid meatballs)

Blanca Paloma is one of those bars where you can feel the atmosphere of the Triana district. You would recognise the place straight away as the corner is always very crowded. Many locals will stop here to have a beer and chat with their friends and relatives.

As in many places, once inside you can stay at the tapas area or ask for a seat in the main room where only big portions can be ordered. In Blanca Paloma you will find traditional food. The selected dish in this place is the squid meatball, a very typical dish along the coasts of Huelva and Cádiz. The secret of cooking meatballs with fish is adding a generous amount of breadcrumbs to create compact balls. Then the cooks will deep-fry and slow cook them with a sauce of vegetables and a reduction of wine. The result is really flavourful and I would recommend them to anybody visiting.

Casa Diego

Address: Esperanza de Triana, 19
Area: Triana
Opening days: Every day
Opening times: 12.30pm – 4pm & 8pm – midnight
Type: Tapas
What to order: Snails

Gastronomy in Seville is very diverse and the reason to include Casa Diego in this book is a very special tapa served here: snails. The bar itself is small and can be noisy, with just a few high tables outside and divided into two parts. Snails can be found in many bars around the city, but it is not always easy to find the best places. The recipe is almost the same at every place; the secret is washing the snails very carefully and then cooking them in a broth with spices.

The snails –*caracoles* in Spanish- of Casa Diego are considered the best in Triana, and even if you have never tried them, you should give it a go. Snails are not served all year round though as the season will only be between April and July. They have another bar in Alfarería Street, closer to the city centre where you can try the same tapas.

El Rinconcillo

Address: Calle Gerona, 40
Area: Santa Catalina
Opening days: Every day
Opening times: 1pm – 1am
Type: Tapas / Restaurant
What to order: Spinach with chickpeas

El Rinconcillo has the privilege of being the oldest bar in Seville. It was founded in 1670 and it is still one of the most popular corners in the city. The same family has run the business since the 19th century and some of the recipes of the meals served here have been passed from generation to generation. You can stay at the tapas area or take a seat in the restaurant room; the experience will be awesome wherever you decide to have your meal.

My selection for this place is spinach with chickpeas, one of the dishes with Arab heritage, very different from the typical Spanish food. Cumin will be the secret ingredient, a spice used commonly in the Middle East. This dish became very popular after the Christian conquest of the south of Spain and is usually prepared during Lent, after the prohibition of eating meat. Don't hesitate and try it!

Mercado de Triana

Address: Plaza del Altozano
Area: Triana
Opening days: Every day
Opening times: Monday - Saturday 9am – midnight Sunday 12pm – 5pm
Type: Market
What to order: Iberian ham

The traditional market of the district of Triana is one of the social centres of the neighbourhood. It is located just across Isabel II Bridge in Plaza del Altozano. This is a traditional market where fresh products are sold on a daily basis, but also a gastronomic centre. Apart from visiting the different shops of the market, at the end of it you will have bars where you can get some tapas or a whole meal.

The fish served here is usually very fresh and tasty, but the selected product in this market is the Iberian ham, one of the star products in Spain. You can get some at the stand of *La Jamonería* or in any of the bars or local shops. The price and quality will depend on the percentage of Iberian breed, as well as the amount of acorns used to feed the animal. The market holds the ruins of St. George's castle, former site of the inquisition.

Affordable Options

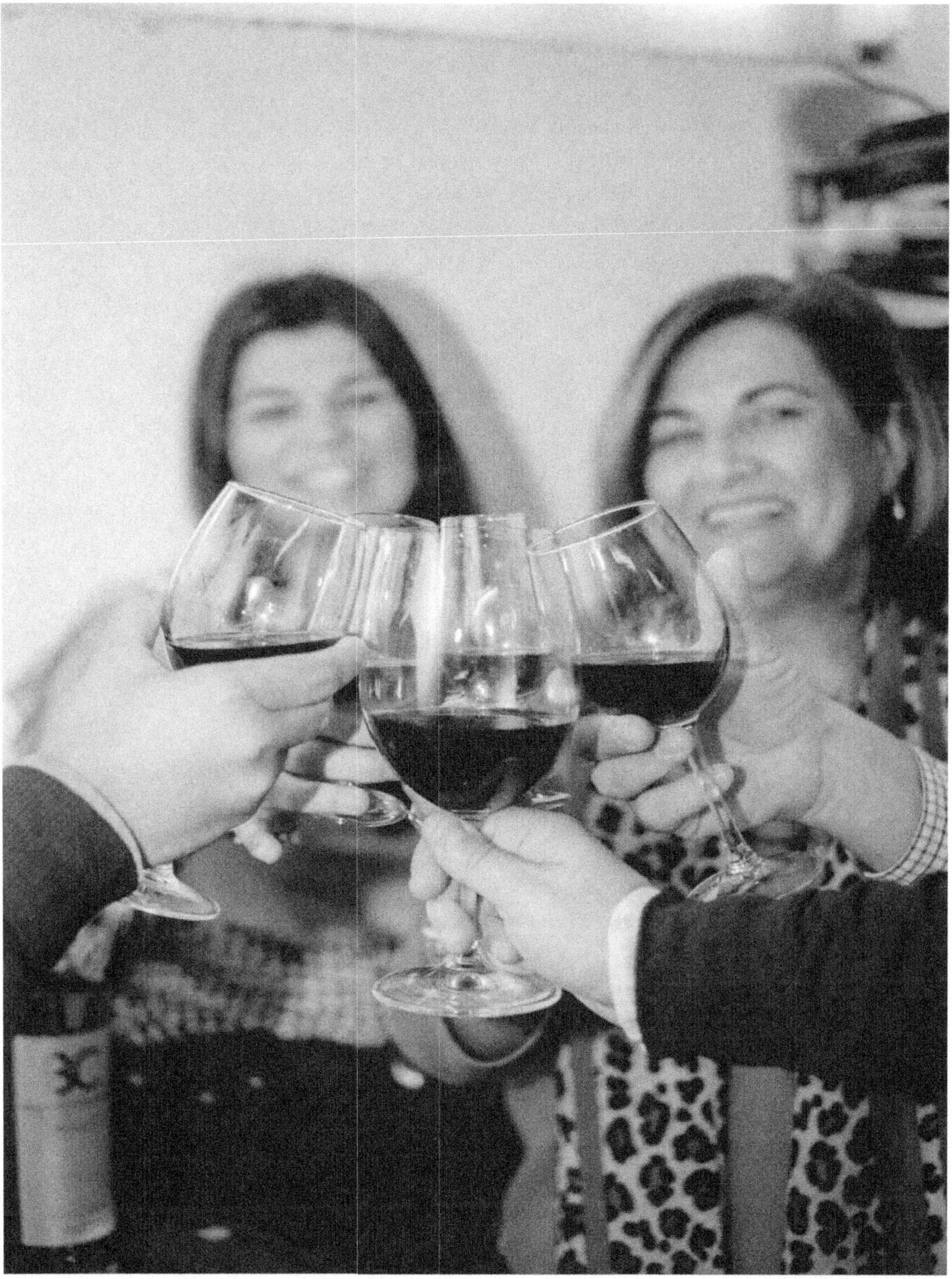

Taberna Coloniales II

Address: Calle Fernández y González, 36
Area: Arenal
Opening days: Every day
Opening times: 12.30pm – 12.15am
Type: Tapas
What to order: Solomillo al whisky

Los Coloniales is a typical tavern very popular among young visitors and students. It offers very good value for money and it is usually very crowded. Unfortunately you cannot book a table in advance, so you will have to show up and ask to be included in the list to get a table. In the meantime you can drink something at the bar. The service is fast and efficient and hopefully in a few minutes you will be seated.

The menu is very diverse, with lots of tapas, half and full portions. My recommendation at Los Coloniales is a dish called *solomillo al whisky,* a pork loin fillet with a sauce consisting of garlic, lemon, wine and whisky. This dish is usually served with potato chips and the portions are generous.

If you are in the area of San Pedro you can go to the second Coloniales located in Plaza del Cristo de Burgos.

Bar Alfalfa

Address: Calle Candilejo, 1
Area: Alfalfa
Opening days: Every day
Opening times: 9am – midnight
Type: Tapas
What to order: Salmorejo

Bar Alfalfa is one of those traditional places with affordable tapas for your stay in Seville (less than €3). Located at Alfalfa Square, you can sit outside and enjoy a wonderful meal. The menu has a lot of Italian influences, with bruschettas, cheeses and different salads.

The tapa I have chosen here is very Andalusian though and it is called *salmorejo*. This improved version of gazpacho is one of the favourite local dishes. A summer recipe, it is now present all year round at every bar or restaurant, both as a main course or as a side. With just a handful of ingredients (tomato, garlic, olive oil, bread, vinegar) you can taste the flavours of the Andalusian countryside.

Salmorejo is served cold and with hardboiled egg and Iberian ham diced on top.

Patio San Eloy

Address: Calle San Eloy, 9
Area: Duque / Campana
Opening days: Every day
Opening times: 12pm – 4.30pm & 7pm – 11.30pm
Type: Tapas
What to order: Montadito Sevillano

El Patio San Eloy was founded in 1972 by a local family. With the decades the family-run business has been growing, becoming one of the greatest companies of the catering industry in Seville. Patio San Eloy now has 12 bars in Seville with the same menu, apart from other restaurants and shops, but this would be the original.

The meals served are not very elaborate and they consist of fried fish, cold tapas, small sandwiches and Iberian meats. I have chosen the small sandwich called *montadito Sevillano*, it could not be any other. This small sandwich is filled with red bell peppers and a frigate tuna fillet, very common in the south west of Spain. You can have your meal seated on the stools at the end of the bar, not the most comfortable spot, but good to enjoy a drink and a tapa.

Taberna del Arenal

Address: Calle Almirante Lobo, 2
Area: Puerta de Jerez
Opening days: Every day
Opening times: 1pm – 4.30pm & 8pm – midnight
Type: Tapas
What to order: Solomillo a la carbonara

This bar is located just two steps away from Puerta de Jerez and Torre del Oro. It has a few tables outside and a big room in the interior. As many popular places in the city, it does not accept bookings, so you will have to be patient, ask to be listed and wait for your table to be ready. It is recommended to go there early, before 2pm for lunch or 9pm for dinner. Prices are very reasonable for the amount of food and its central location, so mainly at the weekend many locals would go here for lunch.

The dish chosen here is called *solomillo a la carbonara*, a pork loin fillet with a version of carbonara sauce. It would not be the same you have in your pasta, but mainly diced bacon, cream and gratin cheese. Be careful when you order as the portions are very generous, so two tapas per person depending on what you order should be enough.

La Antigua Bodeguita

Address: Plaza del Salvador, 6
Area: El Salvador
Opening days: Tuesday to Sunday
Opening times: 12.30pm – 4.30pm & 7.30pm – midnight
Type: Drinks
What to order: Cruzcampo beer

Although it has a name, locals will know this bar simply as the bar of Salvador Square. It is divided into two parts with two bars connected inside and it can be found under the porch of the square. To be honest nobody comes here to eat but to drink. This is a very common meeting point for locals to drink something before lunch or dinner. The bar has lots of high tables in the square and people will share them. It does not have floor staff and you will have to go to the bar any time you need to order, be patient and enjoy the atmosphere around you.

What to order? Just beer. *Caña* is the small beer size served in Seville (half a pint) and this is one of the bars that sells more of these *cañas* in all of Spain. The beer brand in Seville is Cruzcampo, loved by locals.

Las Columnas

Address: Alameda de Hércules, 19
Area: Alameda
Opening days: Every day
Opening times: 7am – midnight
Type: Tapas
What to order: Anchovies marinated in vinegar

Las Columnas is another traditional bar that has maintained its cuisine and prices despite the increase of tourism in the city. It is located in the huge Alameda Square, with many tables outside to enjoy the weather and an amazing atmosphere.

The food served here is mainly Mediterranean, with lots of salads and cold dishes, as well as fish cooked in different ways. The dish chosen for Las Columnas is called *boquerones en vinagre.* The fresh anchovies must be cleaned before and then are marinated with minced garlic, olive oil and of course vinegar. Anchovies sometimes do not have a good reputation, but in Seville you will discover there are different ways of cooking them, all delicious.

This bar is opened almost all day long, so if you are staying in the area, it can be a good spot for a typical Andalusian breakfast too.

Modern Cuisine

Perro Viejo Tapas

Address: Calle Arguijo, 3
Area: Encarnación
Opening days: Every day
Opening times: 1.30pm – 4pm & 8.15pm – midnight
Type: Tapas / Restaurant
What to order: Tuna ceviche

Perro Viejo brings modern techniques and exotic products at an affordable price to the food scene in Seville. The combination of this modernity with top quality local products results in one of the trendiest spots in the city centre. The decor is very well looked after in a rustic style.

The menu is diverse, with some interpretations of the most typical Spanish cuisine recipes with the addition of new ingredients or techniques, mainly Asian origin. The dish I have chosen is the *tuna ceviche*, marinated with citrus juices, a flavourful option and very different from the traditional Spanish cuisine.

Perro Viejo is also famous for its desserts; do not miss the chance of trying their version of *torrija*, a sweet made of bread eaten during Lent time. Perro Viejo opened a smaller place nearby called Perro Chiko.

Ovejas Negras Tapas

Address: Calle Hernando Colón, 8
Area: Monumental area
Opening days: Every day
Opening times: 1pm – 4.30pm & 8.30pm – 11.30pm
Type: Tapas / Restaurant
What to order: Risottazo

Ovejas Negras is the perfect choice for your stay in Seville. The venue is simply beautiful and every detail is well looked after. It is located in Calle Hernando Colón, between the cathedral and the city hall. The attention and availability of the staff is also a strong point of this place, as is of course the quality of its food, having the privilege of a mention in the Michelin guide.

The menu is not a never-ending list, but a carefully selected amount of tapas and dishes. It combines traditional products of Andalusia with pinches of modernity. The food is very good value for money and it is easy to understand how difficult it is to get a table. There is a board outside where they write down your name and amount of people. When it is your turn, they will accompany you to your table. *Risottazo* is my choice for this spot, served with a cream of boletus (a wild mushroom) and cherry tomatoes, just awesome.

Lobo López

Address: Calle Rosario, 15
Area: Monumental area
Opening days: Every day
Opening times: Monday to Friday 8am – 11.30pm
Weekends 9am – 11.30pm
Type: Tapas / Restaurant
What to order: Hot lobster

This is one of the trendiest venues in modern gastronomical Seville. The place itself is very big, with three separate spaces. The tropical plants, the mirrors, the wooden ceilings and the open kitchen like a typical patio of Seville create the ideal atmosphere for the perfect dinner.

The floor is very big at Lobo López and it is not difficult to get a table. I would only recommend calling in advance if you are a big group.

The menu, as in many modern cuisine places, is not too large but features the best from local and exotic cuisine. The hot lobster is the star dish in this restaurant, and the interpretation of the hot dog will add a different taste to your stay in Seville. The cocktails are also a strong point in Lobo López, do not miss the opportunity to try some.

Eslava

Address: Calle Eslava, 3
Area: San Lorenzo
Opening days: Tuesday to Sunday
Opening times: Tuesday to Saturday 12.30pm – midnight
Sundays 12.30pm – 5pm
Type: Tapas / Restaurant
What to order: Egg yolk on boletus (a wild mushroom) & truffle sponge

Eslava is probably the best known modern cuisine restaurant in Seville city centre. Located near Plaza de San Lorenzo, it has earned a very good reputation due to the service offered and the quality of its meals. It is one of the 21 places in Seville mentioned in the Michelin Guide.

This is one of those venues where you will have to wait if you want to eat at the time of locals, so I would recommend that you show up early. The cuisine here is traditional with innovation in its techniques. The star dish here is the egg yolk on boletus and truffle sponge, a small bite with an explosion of flavours in the mouth. A must-try if you visit Seville. Desserts in Eslava are also very good, especially the cured cheese ice cream.

La Bernarda Slowbar

Address: Calle Juan de Mata Carriazo
Area: San Bernardo
Opening days: Every day
Opening times: 1.30pm – midnight
Type: Restaurant
What to order: Grilled octopus with mashed potatoes

This is one of the few venues located out of the former city walls included in this book. Located in San Bernardo district, just a short walk from the city centre, La Bernarda has become a very popular spot in the last few years.

The place is massive but it can be full sometimes, so it is recommended to go there early. You can sit outside or in the big room. There are some high tables too for a more informal dinner. The appearance is very tropical with decorative plants all over the place. Its menu offers a wide variety of salads and cold dishes, top quality fish and grilled meats. Despite the decor and high quality of the meals, prices are still very reasonable.

Don't miss the grilled octopus, served with mashed potatoes, paprika and extra virgin olive oil.

Tradevo Centro

Address: Calle Cuesta del Rosario, 15
Area: Alfalfa
Opening days: Every day
Opening times: 1pm – 4.30pm & 8.45pm – 11.30pm
Type: Tapas / Restaurant
What to order: Marinated sardine

Tradevo is one of the venues in Seville with a mention in the Michelin Guide and totally deserved. It is located off Plaza del Salvador, at a perfect corner where you can enjoy a wonderful meal. The place inside is not very big and the tables are small, but you can sit outside to enjoy the weather in Seville.

This place offers both tapas and full portions in some of the dishes; I would recommend that you order portions to share. Although the cost of a meal is slightly higher than the average in similar places, the quality and service are well worth the money.

The dish chosen for Tradevo is the marinated sardine with tomato bread toast and roast peppers. It can be ordered by unit, as a tapa or as a full portion to share. After the success of this and other dishes, Tradevo has opened other venues in areas like San Bernardo.

High Standards

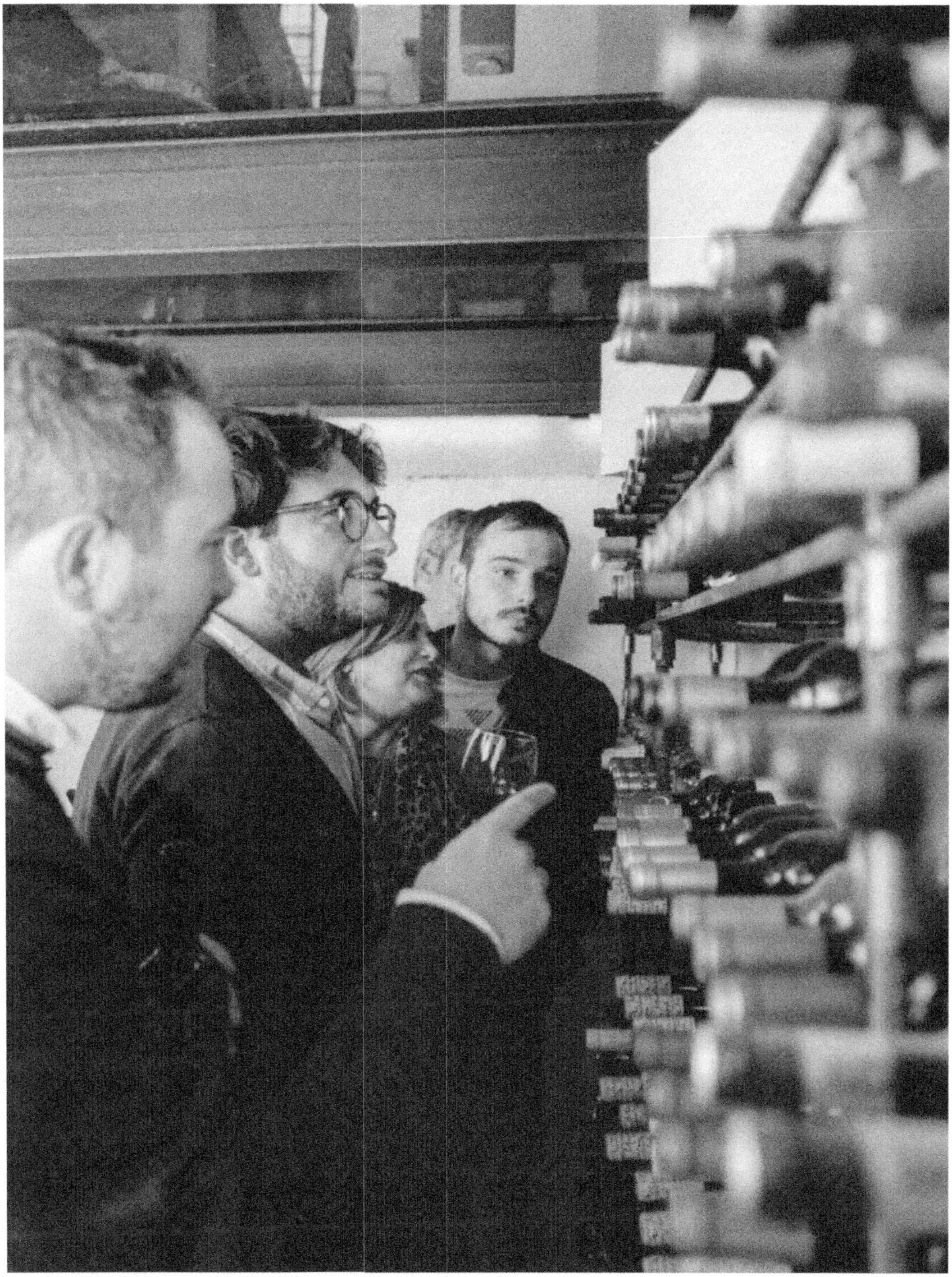

Azahar

Address: Plaza Jesús de la Redención, 2
Area: Alfalfa
Opening days: Every day
Opening times: 1.30pm – 3.30pm & 8pm – 11pm
Type: Restaurant
What to order: Salmon loin on papillote

Azahar is the restaurant of a luxurious boutique hotel called Hospes Las Casas del Rey de Baeza, located at a former noble house in the heart of Seville. The restaurant occupies the patio of the former house and a room next to it, where it is possible to enjoy a meal with the authentic Andalusian atmosphere. Due to the reduced space and availability, please book in advance if you are planning to go. The cuisine here is still traditional with modern techniques, but its prices will match more with a haute cuisine restaurant.

Once you get there and have a look at the menu, you can choose whether to go for the tasting menu or order directly from the general menu. If you do so, here is my recommendation; salmon loin on papillote and coriander oil and lime.

Bajo guía

Address: Calle Adriano, 5
Area: Arenal
Opening days: Tuesday to Sunday
Opening times: 12pm – 5pm & 8.30pm – midnight
Type: Restaurant
What to order: Prawns

This venue was opened in 2007 in the Arenal district of Seville city centre. Having its origin in Sanlúcar de Barrameda in Cádiz province, the owners decided to bring their products to the capital. The appearance of the restaurant is kind of old fashioned, like what you can find in their coast venues.

The menu is very focused on fish and seafood, cooked in different ways; boiled, grilled or fried. All the products offered in Bajo Guía are from the region and extremely fresh and the prices are according to the market, even if not affordable for every budget. I have chosen shrimps as the must try in this restaurant. Shrimps and prawns from Huelva and Cádiz province are very coveted and good quality can be around €150 per kilo already cooked and served to a table. Beware! Prawns are served with shells and you will have to peel them.

Taberna del Alabardero

Address: Calle Zaragoza, 20
Area: Monumental area
Opening days: Tuesday to Sunday
Opening times: 1pm – 4pm & 7.30pm – 11am
Type: Restaurant
What to order: Mellow rice with squid

Taberna del Alabardero is a classic restaurant in Seville city centre. Located at a 19th century stately house, it hosts a boutique hotel, a restaurant, a café and tapas lounge, a terrace and a culinary centre, where local students train to become professional chefs.

The decor is traditional as well as the layout of the tables along the different rooms. The menu is not very long, with more starter options than main courses. You can always order more starters to share if you want to try different things. One of these starters is the mellow rice with squid, a classic dish you can find in many places in Spain, but in this case innovated by adding a coconut and ink aioli, really tasty and a good point to start from. After, there are some fish and meat you can try to make your stay in Taberna del Alabardero memorable.

Abantal

Address: C/ Alcalde José de la Bandera, 7
Area: San Bernardo
Opening days: Tuesday to Sunday
Opening times: 2pm – 4pm & 8.30pm – 10.30pm
Type: Restaurant
What to order: Tasting menu

Abantal is probably the best restaurant in Seville city. It has been recognised with a Michelin star due to the creativity of Chef Julio Fernández Quintero. Its capacity is small, about 28 people for each service and it is recommended to book before arriving Seville. The prices for a tasting menu go from €80 to €115.

Going to Abantal is an experience for all your senses; you will discover new textures and flavours always with the top quality products of the Andalusian region, highlighting the extra virgin olive oils. Avant-garde cuisine is brought to its maximum here as you can book the chef's table, located in the kitchen. You will discover in first person how all the dishes are created and will see how the job is done at a haute cuisine restaurant kitchen.

Casa Manolo León

Address: Calle Guadalquivir, 8
Area: San Lorenzo
Opening days: Tuesday to Sunday
Opening times: 1.30pm – 5.30pm & 8pm – 1.30am
Type: Restaurant
What to order: Red tuna dices

Located at a 19th century stately house, this restaurant was opened in 1999. Since then its reputation has grown and it is considered nowadays to be one of the best restaurants in the city. The house is divided into two floors with four internal spaces and patios. It is much recommended to have a look at the green house and if possible, ask for a table in this space. The decoration maintains the appearance of the 19th century house with historical paintings and bright colours. The main products are very local with the introduction of some ingredients with diverse origins and avant-garde techniques.

The dish I have chosen for this place is the red tuna dices. These are served marinated with soy and ginger with a side of red rice and soy mayonnaise.

Abades Triana

Address: Calle Betis
Area: Triana
Opening days: Every day
Opening times: 1.30pm – 4pm & 8.30pm – 1.30am
Type: Restaurant
What to order: Arborio rice with Iberian pork loin

Abades Triana is a restaurant with a privileged view over the river and city of Seville. Located on the Guadalquivir shore, it has an amazing terrace with a relaxed atmosphere, perfect to enjoy a wonderful meal.

Abades is part of a huge chain with hotels and restaurants all over Andalusia that has been running for more than 25 years. The main ingredients of all dishes served here are top quality Andalusian products and that is noticeable in the taste of the dishes. The menu changes every six months, but the star dish is the Arborio rice with Iberian pork loin, truffles and boletus. This is a version of the Italian risotto with Iberian products and the special pinch of lime zest. Not to be missed!

Río Grande

Address: Calle Betis
Area: Triana
Opening days: Every day
Opening times: 1pm – 4pm & 7.30pm – 11.30pm
Type: Restaurant
What to order: Steak tartare

Rio Grande is one of the most luxurious restaurants in Seville. The view from this venue of Torre del Oro across the river and the whole city of Seville, together with the very well looked after rooms and garden, create the ideal atmosphere.

The menu is much more extensive than what is typical for a high end restaurant, with many options from the countryside, livestock and mainly the sea. The Chef Fran Trigo is constantly innovating in techniques and new ingredients, becoming one of the greatest in the city.

One of the delicacies served here is the steak tartare. The steak from famous Galician veal comes with powder of sweet extra virgin olive oil, egg yolk and textured capers. Totally worth the experience!

Barbiana

Address: Calle Albareda, 11
Area: Monumental area
Opening days: Monday to Saturday
Opening times: 12.30pm – 4.30pm & 8.30pm – midnight
Type: Tapas / Restaurant
What to order: Shrimp omelettes

Barbiana is located in the monumental area of the city, just off Plaza Nueva. It brings to Seville the flavours of the coast of Sanlúcar de Barrameda, Cádiz and its *Manzanilla,* a kind of sherry wine originally from this village. This family run business is preserving that traditional essence since 1986.

At Barbiana you can stay at the bar and order just a glass of wine and an appetizer or ask for a table in the room to enjoy a full meal. The menu is very focused on seafood and fish, as well as rices. I have chosen a classic recipe from the Cádiz area. Although it is called omelette, it has no eggs but dough made of wheat flour, chickpea flour and parsley. You can order them by unit or as a full portion to share. A must-try during your stay in Andalusia.

Lonja del Barranco

Address: Calle Arjona, 28
Area: River
Opening days: Every day
Opening times: Sunday to Thursday 10am – midnight
Friday & Saturday 10am – 2am
Type: Market / Tapas
What to order: Fried fish

This gourmet market was opened in 2014 and attracts over a million visitors a year. It occupies the structure that used to host the fish market of the city and it is a symbol of the iron architecture of the 19th century in Seville, together with Triana Bridge.

Inside the market there are over 20 stands with a different culinary offer. You can taste rices, meats, fish and seafood, but also dishes from foreign cuisines as Mexican, Italian or Japanese

The prices are higher than those you can find at other bars and restaurants around the city for similar quality products. As a must try, I have chosen fried fish in here. The fish shop of the market also works as a *freiduría* and you can order your fish to eat it straight away over a beer or wine. The pleasant atmosphere is really worth a visit during your stay in Seville.

Ena

Address: Calle San Fernando, 2
Area: Monumental area
Opening days: Every day
Opening times: 1pm – 4pm & 8pm – 11.30pm
Type: Tapas
What to order: Artichoke flowers with romesco sauce

This is one of the three restaurants of the luxurious Alfonso XIII Hotel. It is located in the terrace, the most informal area of the restaurant, with a tropical design and amazing views. The menu was designed by the Michelin star award winning chef, Carles Abellán and combines the best of the Catalan and Andalusian cuisines.

The dish chosen here is the artichoke flower with romesco sauce. This sauce is Catalan in origin with tomato, seeds, bread, garlic and dried red peppers. For a full meal you will need more than a tapa, and that is great to have the chance to try other interpretations of traditional recipes like *salmorejo*. The terrace is open non-stop from 1pm to 11.30pm and you can go and have a drink at any time. The kitchen schedule is the one specified in the description.

FLAMENCO AMONG LOCALS

It would be very difficult to understand Seville without flamenco and to understand flamenco without Seville. Flamenco was listed by Unesco as Intangible World Heritage in 2010, but its origin is still a subject of debate. Many will exclusively refer to the gipsy population that arrived in the Iberian Peninsula during the first third of the 15th century, and of course they played an important role, but it could not be understood without the contribution of other social groups. There were gypsies in other regions of Spain and in other European countries, but the folklore that resulted in flamenco only emerged in the south of Spain. The importance of other groups, such as the Moorish or Sephardic Jews, cannot be discounted, as well as the Castilian traditions of singing romances during the Middle Age.

Flamenco and folklore have become one more tourist attraction for people visiting Seville, but they are part of locals' social lives too. One of the greatest events in the city is the April Fair, celebrated two weeks after Easter, becoming the greatest exponent of popular culture.

During that week, locals will gather at an enclosure consisting of over 1,000 *casetas*, tents with a bar where we eat, drink, dance and sing. Most of these tents are private and they belong to associations, families, clubs or companies and only members and their guests can access them. That is probably why it is not recommended to visit the April Fair if you do not have a contact in the city. You will be amazed by the horses, colours, dresses of women and suits of men, but you will not be able to be an active part of it. The music performed during this celebration is mainly *sevillanas,* the typical dance from Seville, danced in pairs in four different stages. Every party in the city will have a bit of this; it does not matter if it is a wedding, a Christmas party or a barbecue at a friend's house. The dance of *sevillanas* is not very professional, and even if there are some steps, people will learn by looking and imitating.

The rest of the year, locals will gather in some places that always have this atmosphere. These are the places where you can immerse yourself like a local. These are generally bars, where you can see a short show or where customers will simply start singing, playing instruments and dancing. Obviously you will always have the opportunity to go to a well-prepared show while in Seville. Flamenco has become more professional in the last decades and the performers you will see at the shows have studied for years at the best dance conservatories all over Spain.

Every second year during September and October, Seville hosts a biennial about flamenco with shows in different theatres, outdoors stages and venues where the best performers will demonstrate their skills. Flamenco in Seville is very linked to the Triana district, considered by many experts as the epicentre of this genre. What cannot be debated is that flamenco is one of the distinguishing symbols of our culture and history, not only in Seville or Andalusia, but also beyond our borders.

In this chapter I will try to share real folklore and flamenco with potential visitors to Seville. These places are just bars, with free access where you can enjoy the atmosphere while having a drink and chatting with locals. I hope you enjoy this part of Seville and do not forget to say *OLE* after every song!

Triana

Casa la Anselma

Address: Calle Pagés del Corro, 49
Opening days: Monday to Saturday
Opening times: 11.45pm – 2.30am
Type: Bar / Nightlife
Best days to go: Friday and Saturday

This is the house of Anselma, a typical bar where flamenco is performed. The place is decorated with images of saints and the Virgin of Triana, bullfighters and ceramic originals from this special neighbourhood. It is also interesting to see the commemorative posters of the different editions of the April Fair or the spring celebrations, including Holy Week.

It is highly recommended to book a table in advance not to miss anything about the show. Entry is free of charge, but there is a minimum consumption per person of €7 if you book a table. Apart from the show you will enjoy how attendants will clap, sing and dance on the breaks. Nightlife in Seville starts really late and Casa Anselma is only opening its doors at almost midnight. If you want to feel like a real local, you will have to stay there until closing time.

Bar El Rejoneo

Address: Calle Betis, 31B
Opening days: Thursday to Saturday
Opening times: 11pm – 4.30am
Type: Bar / Nightlife
Best days to go: Friday and Saturday

Rejoneo is located in Calle Betis, next to a very similar venue called Lo Nuestro, on the river shore of Triana. This bar opens at night as a flamenco specialised club. The decor is a bit different than the usual; a bit sober with only some paintings of countryside landscapes displayed.

There is a live show that I would recommend to attend. To do so, you will have to get there early, before midnight to get a nice spot. After some *sevillanas* and other folklore musical pieces are played, people will sing and dance all night long. There is no ticket charge to get into the bar, so you will only pay for your drinks. Beers, wines and cocktails are served here until 4.30am. Cocktails are priced around €7-€9, a bit more than the average in the city, but well worth it due to the wonderful atmosphere.

The bar also opens in the afternoon from 5pm on certain weekends offering live shows too.

Lo Nuestro Flamenco

Address: Calle Betis, 31
Opening days: Thursday to Saturday
Opening times: 11pm – 5.30am
Type: Bar / Nightlife
Best days to go: Friday and Saturday

Lo Nuestro is one of those places very well known by locals who look forward to dancing and singing like in the April Fair. Mainly *sevillanas* and rumbas will entertain hundreds of customers in a very festive atmosphere. You will feel like you were in one of the tents of the fair.

The performers are never very professional here, but they would be very lively and really know how to make everybody participate in their show. After observing the *sevillanas* dance, I am sure you will try it with some locals.

The party starts late, so you will have time to have dinner, go for some drinks and get to Lo Nuestro at around midnight. The level of party will increase as the night goes on, and even if most people will just chat with friends and listen to the music early on, sooner or later, everybody will join in.

T de Triana

Address: Calle Betis, 20
Opening days: Every day
Opening times: Monday to Friday 7pm – 2am
Weekends 5pm – 2am
Type: Bar / Tapas
Best days to go: Friday

T de Triana is a typical Andalusian tavern, bringing together some of the locals' passions: football on the big screen when any of the Seville teams are playing, tapas and a flamenco atmosphere all year round. This is a place where you can have dinner and stay all night long. There are a few high tables outside for tapas and then there is a small room inside for the performances, where you will really feel you are part of the show. The decor is reminiscent of an Andalusian country house, with many utensils on the walls and paintings of scenes of the city and landscapes from times gone by.

There are performances on at 9.30pm, sometimes with English language explanations as an attempt to involve curious visitors in the flamenco atmosphere. This is a great approach for those who are having their first experience with this art.

La Taberna

Address: Calle Duarte, 3
Opening days: Every day
Opening times: Monday to Saturday 7pm – 2am
Sunday 7pm – midnight
Type: Bar / Tapas
Best days to go: Weekends

La Taberna is located on a narrow street off Calle Betis and it is another typical place rarely visited by international tourists. Most of the customers are from the neighbourhood, other parts of the city or tourists from other parts of Spain. It is definitely not a tourist trap and you can notice this by its affordable prices.

The furniture of this venue is identical to many of the tents of the April Fair, with low tables and wicker chairs. The decorations on the walls include utensils and old pictures. At the end of the room you will see the very small stage, for the two or three performers to sing and dance. Going to La Taberna is an intimate experience for visitors to Seville to enjoy a drink or tapa surrounded by locals. I would recommend going early if you want to have a seat, it usually gets really crowded.

City Centre

Mariscal Café Español

Address: Calle Mariscal, 3
Opening days: Every day
Opening times: From 8pm
Type: Bar / Drinks
Best days to go: Weekends

Mariscal is located in one of the narrowest streets in Seville city centre, in the former Jewish quarter and two steps away from Murillo Gardens. Its modest entrance will bring you to an authentic flamenco bar. Once inside you will see some marble columns, probably remnants of a disappeared courtyard. As you enter you will see some instruments that are part of every party held inside, such as drum boxes or guitars. The place itself is not very big and the space is reduced for dance. Chairs are usually arranged in a circle to leave space for the dancers in the middle.

The best time to go is from 11pm, when a flamenco show will take place and then let the party just begin. Flamenco should be spontaneous and some of the attendants will suddenly start singing while others clap and dance. Inside, only drinks are served, mainly cocktails. As in many places, the longer you stay, the bigger the party is.

Arfe 11

Address: Calle Arfe, 11
Opening days: Monday to Sunday
Opening times: 1pm – 11pm
Type: Bar / Drinks
Best days to go: Weekends

Arfe11 is one of the places where the younger enthusiasts of flamenco will gather. This bar is really small and sometimes it gets really busy. The advised closing time is 11pm, but at the weekends they will close later.

The name of the place is as easy to remember as its address. Arfe Street has many different bars and is a nice area to walk around and have a drink even if you are not looking for flamenco, due to the different options you will have along the same street.

There are no performers here, but some of the customers will start singing, dancing and playing instruments (honestly some better than others), but it is usually fun. Here you can experience how young locals enjoy flamenco. Beside this venue there is another bar called Casa Matías, with a similar atmosphere.

Quitapesares

Address: Plaza Padre Jerónimo de Córdoba, 3
Opening days: Monday to Saturday
Opening times: 12pm – 4pm & 8.30pm – 1am
Type: Bar / Tapas
Best days to go: Weekends

Quitapesares is known among locals as Peregil Tavern, the reason being that the owner, Pepe Peregil, was a famous flamenco singer. Here, Pepe used to serve his tapas and while he did he sang to his clients some verses of flamenco music. Pepe was the only waiter working here and the place closes on Sundays and in July and August. Around the walls there are many photographs of celebrities of flamenco together with Pepe, who died in 2012.

The food served consists of Iberian meat tapas and its prices are very reasonable. You can also try a good orange wine and *Manzanilla*, directly served from the barrels.

A similar atmosphere can be found at his family other venue closer to the cathedral, at Mateos Gago Street, called Álvaro Peregil.

La Carbonería

Address: Calle Céspedes, 21A
Opening days: Every day
Opening times: 7pm – 2am
Type: Bar / Tapas
Best days to go: Any day

La Carbonería is included in this list more for what it was than for what it is. It has traditionally been a place made by locals for locals, but with the increase in tourism, it has lost part of the essence of real flamenco. Decades ago, this was more like the other places mentioned in this book, really spontaneous. Today, it has become one more tourist attraction in the city, included in every standard guidebook and online platforms.

This venue is located in the former Jewish quarter and despite the small entrance is very big inside, as the main room is a former courtyard. Entry is free of charge and it is recommended to get inside early. They have shows every day and the shows are not too long. It can be a good idea for those who have no idea about flamenco and want to experience it for the first time, but if you want to experience something more authentic, I would recommend looking for other places.

EXPLORING OUTSIDE SEVILLE

Seville is the capital city of Andalusia and has a lot to offer. Most tourists will also visit other capitals in the provinces nearby, like Córdoba, Granada, Cádiz or Málaga, but the areas around these big cities have also a rich heritage that deserves to be better known, and in this book I have selected some of the possible destinations for a day trip out of the urban noise.

The area surrounding Seville shares the history of the capital, the architecture and the artistic styles. Although they have preserved part of the heritage, some of the places we mention in this chapter have lost the importance they had in past periods. Some of these places played an important role during conquests and battles and also were relevant cultural centres.

In this chapter I will give recommendations on what to visit in the different destinations, how to get there and also information about the main monuments.

Itálica

Address: Avenida de Extremadura, 2
Town: Santiponce
Landmark: Archaeological site
Distance: 11 kms (7 miles)
Opening days: Tuesday to Sunday
Visit times: September to March 9am – 6pm
April to June 9am – 8pm
July & August 9am – 3pm
Sundays 9am – 3pm
Price: €1.50 (Free for EU citizens)
Audioguide: Not available
Best transport: Private car
Public bus: Available
Estimated time: 2 hours

Itálica is a Roman city located 11 kms from Seville city centre, in the town of Santiponce. The origins of this city come from the battle of Ilipa (206 BC), when Romans commanded by Scipio defeated Carthaginians in the context of the second Punic War. Ilipa is according to historians located near the village of Alcalá del Río, near Itálica.

Romans took advantage of a Turdetan settlement existing since the 4th century BC and founded what is considered the first Roman city outside of Italy. Itálica became an important trade centre due its proximity to the river and many of the local products of the province were distributed from this city to every corner of the Roman Empire. It reached its highest status during the second century AD as the place of origin of the Emperors Trajan and Hadrian and home town to many of the senators of the time.

The area we can visit nowadays is the one built during the 2nd century, at the time of Emperor Hadrian. This is the part that got abandoned after the arrival of Visigoths, while the other parts of the village exist until today. These areas cannot be visited as they are preserved underneath the houses of Santiponce village.

Itálica, as a powerful trade centre and linked to two emperors, preserved a rich heritage in buildings, utensils, mosaics and sculptures. Some of these remains are kept at the Archaeological Museum of Seville located in Plaza de América. By walking around the streets of Itálica, visitors can understand in a better way the public buildings, houses and objects used on a daily basis during the Roman time. Itálica is nowadays in the process of being listed as World Heritage site by Unesco, a status that would help its preservation.

Recommended Itinerary
- Audiovisual room
- North wall
- Cardo maximus
- House of the exedra
- House of Neptune
- House of the birds
- Baths
- House of the Planetarium
- Amphitheatre

Tips & Info
Itálica is not well connected with the city of Seville and the best way to save time getting there is by private car. If you do not have the option of renting a private car, there is always the possibility of going by public transport. The public bus M-170A leaves Seville from Plaza de Armas bus station every 20 or 30 minutes approximately and after crossing the towns of Camas and

Santiponce has its last stop at the gate of the archaeological site. Some visitors will prefer to get a taxi or an Uber due to its proximity with the capital. The average cost of a one way journey is around €15 - €20. Some companies are offering half day tours to Itálica with pick up and drop off in the city centre and that can be a handy way of getting to the monument.

Once you are there, you will see the small ticket office. Fares are due to be changed, but by May 2020 the ticket price is €1.50. If you are an EU citizen you will have to show your ID or passport and access will be free of charge. As soon as you enter you will see a full map of the site and the old city of Itálica, as well as a building on your right where in an audiovisual room, they project an introductory video.

Unfortunately there is no possibility of renting any audio guide on site and the panels displayed can be confusing. They are not very well looked after and it is difficult to understand the different buildings and mosaics around the site. It would be a pity walking around this beautiful complex without any source of information. I strongly recommend visiting the archaeological site of Itálica with a licensed guide not to miss any detail and to enjoy an immersive experience. You should contact a guide in advance as it is very difficult to find any available around the monument.

Do not miss the amazing mosaics of Neptune, the birds and the planetarium, as well as the amphitheatre. The amphitheatre of Itálica was built approximately between 117 & 138 AD at the time of Emperor Hadrian out of the city walls of Itálica. It was one of the largest in the whole empire with a capacity of over 25,000 spectators. These spectators would be distributed in three levels of a stand around the elliptical shaped arena. In the middle there is a pit for the different shows, such as gladiators, like in the Colosseum in Rome.

Itálica, like other parts of the province of Seville, was chosen as a set for the successful TV series Game of Thrones, as the amphitheatre called the Dragon Pit.

Seville is a hot city and on a visit to Itálica you will not have many chances of hiding from the sun. I would recommend that you come and visit early in the morning to avoid the warmest hours. At the end of your visit you can also stop at the village of Santiponce for a walk and visit the Roman Theatre. This theatre is not in the archaeological site, but in the middle of the village, just a few minutes' walk. Do not forget to stop for a drink and a tapa in this village and the bar in front of the entrance of the archaeological site is a good option for it.

A visit to Itálica is mandatory for everybody interested in Roman history and heritage. The place receives more visitors due to the quality of the mosaics and the uniqueness of the preserved buildings. Hopefully with its declaration as a World Heritage site, it will get more investment for its preservation.

Monastery of Saint Isidoro del Campo

Address: Avenida de San Isidoro 18
Town: Santiponce
Landmark: Monastery
Distance: 10 kms (6 miles)
Opening days: Wednesday to Sunday
Visit times: 10am – 2pm (every day)
Fridays and Saturdays also afternoon:
October - March 4pm – 7pm
April - Sept 5.30pm – 8.30 pm
Price: Free
Audioguide: Not available
Best transport: Private car
Public bus: Available
Estimated time: 1 hour

Saint Isidoro Monastery is located just outside Seville in the village of Santiponce. It was founded in 1301 at a place close to the Roman ruins of Itálica, where according to the tradition Saint Isidoro had been buried. Its founders were Alonso Pérez de Guzmán and María Alonso Coronel, who built it as a family pantheon too. Throughout the centuries it has been under the administration of different religious orders like Cistercians, Observant Hieronymites and the order of Saint Jerome.

The monastery was built in Gothic Mudéjar style with defensive elements due to its location. The church consists of two Gothic naves, the second one built by the son of Alfonso Pérez de Guzmán. The altarpieces of the church are a work of one of the greatest Seville Baroque masters, Juan Martínez Montañés. The older nave functioned as a monastic church, while the newer one was the parish church.

The monastery has two Mudéjar cloisters decorated with frescos from different periods. Around these you can access some areas like the refectory, with Gothic vaults and paintings from the late 15th century. The sacristy and the chapter house will also have an entrance from the main cloister, called Cloister of the Dead, as it work as a cemetery.

This monastery was active until 1835, when it became state property after the ecclesiastical confiscation of Mendizábal. No use was given to it and the passage of the decades damaged the structures of the complex. The building was extensively restored in 2002 and is now heritage and property of the Autonomous Community of Andalusia.

Recommended Itinerary
- Orange Tree Courtyard
- Choir
- Cloister of the Dead
- Cloister of the Evangelists
- Refectory
- Sacristy and Chapterhouse
- Chamber of the Reservation
- Presbytery of the Church
- Second church

Tips & Info

The Monastery of Saint Isidoro del Campo is one of the most impressive and unknown religious buildings of the province of Seville. It was built after the Christian conquest of Seville and also worked as a fortress. After the restoration works of 2002, it is now as astonishing as it was before being abandoned in 1835. This visit poses a big surprise to those visitors that come to Santiponce to visit the Roman city of Itálica and enter just to have a look.

Getting here is not an easy duty though. The best way would be by car, but if you are not renting a car while in Andalusia there are some alternatives. There is a public bus from Plaza de Armas station to Santiponce, numbered M-170A. The stop is in the big avenue that crosses the village and you will have to walk for around five minutes to get to the monastery. The last option would be getting a taxi or an Uber that would cost around €15-€20 each way. Some of the companies offering half day tours to Itálica would also include a visit to the monastery.

As the entrance is free of charge (by May 2020), once you are there you just need to tell your place of origin, for the database and you will be free to explore. There is no audio guide available, nor even the possibility of hiring any licensed guide on site, so it is highly recommended to contact any guide or agency in advance or to bring a source of information with you. You can also buy the official book at the entrance to follow.

In some of the rooms of the monastery you will see some remains of Roman busts and columns originally from Itálica. Some of these materials were recycled during the construction of the monastery.

This place has over 700 years of history and many important things happened within its walls. During the 16th century, it became one of the origins of the Reformation in Spain. Inside this monastery, monks read and translated some of the books forbidden by the Inquisition. Some of the monks where executed while others could escape to other European countries. That is the case of Casiodoro de Reina, who first translated the Bible to Spanish in 1569, known as the Bear Bible.

Do not miss the Chamber of the Reservation, the most holy place in the monastery, with sculptures of the Virgin with child, Saint Joachim and Saint Anne by Martínez Montañés.

The visit to the monastery takes about one hour and is the perfect combination for a visit to Itálica, spending a whole morning at the village of Santiponce. This will enrich your knowledge about medieval history, Mudéjar architecture and Baroque sculpture.

Carmona

Landmarks: Roman necropolis & old town
Distance: 35 kms (22 miles)
Best transport: Private car
Public bus: Available
Estimated time: Half a day

Carmona is a village located in the countryside about 35 kms from Seville with a population of 30,000 inhabitants. Carmona has been occupied for 5,000 years. It was probably one of the fortified cities of the kingdom of Tartessos, then occupied by Phoenicians, Romans, Visigoths, Muslims and Christians.

The importance of Carmona first comes from its location; on a hill in the Guadalquivir River Valley was the perfect place to dominate the territories around. Out of the old city, Carmona hosts one of the best preserved Roman ruins in Andalusia, the Necropolis.

The Necropolis of Carmona was used during the 1st and 2nd century AD. The Necropolis has many chambers excavated in the rock, with niches for urns around it. The outside parts of many of these family pantheons have disappeared due to plunders throughout the centuries. Next to them there are crematoriums where the last part of the funeral rituals took part. Some of the tombs are very ornate, such as one that is called the Elephant and Servilia's Tomb.

Another important part of Carmona is the old town, located between the Gate of Seville and the Gate of Cordoba. These are two of the entrances to the old city very well preserved. The Gate of Seville was built as a fortress in different periods, the oldest part originally from the 9th century BC. The old town is full of narrow streets with just a few squares opened. The most important is Plaza de San Fernando, where it is believed the former Roman forum was located. There are interesting stately houses, convents and churches with a very rich heritage. The church of Saint Mary was built in the 1400s at a location once occupied by one of the mosques of Carmona, preserving parts of the ablutions courtyard.

Carmona also has an interesting Alcázar built by King Peter I during the 1360s, known as the upper alcázar, on the top of the hill. The monument probably has a Moorish origin, and was then used after the Christian conquest. Peter I refurnished it in Mudéjar style and chose Carmona as one of his favourite residences. It was seriously damaged in two earthquakes until in 1976 it was restored to become a Parador; a luxurious hotel property of the state at a historical location.

Recommended Itinerary
- Roman Necropolis
  - Gate of Seville
  - Gate of Córdoba
  - Church of Saint Mary
  - Plaza de San Fernando
  - Market
  - Alcázar

Tips & Info

Carmona is a lovely city to walk around and locals are very welcoming and helpful with visitors. The only public transport available is the bus, as trains do not go to this beautiful town. Buses depart from San Bernardo every hour, but it will take over an hour to get to Carmona due to the numerous stops. It is highly recommended to rent a car if you are planning to visit. It could be an interesting stop if you are thinking of spending a day in Córdoba too.

Once you get to Carmona, the first stop should be the Roman Necropolis. Just opposite the entrance you will see the remains of the Roman amphitheatre that can be seen from outside, but unfortunately not visited. The access to the Necropolis at May 2020 is €1.50 (free for EU citizens). The rooms around the ticket office must be your first stop inside to understand the archaeological site you are going to visit. There are interesting information panels and audiovisual resources as well as some of the objects found during the excavation campaigns. Do not miss the chance of getting into some of the chambers using the ladders and exploring the interior of the tombs. After about 45 minutes you should be done at the Necropolis and it would be time to go to the old town of Carmona.

If you get to Carmona by car, you should park around the Alameda while you visit the Gate of Seville. Near this location there is the Church of Saint Peter, with a similar bell tower to the Giralda, in Seville. By the Gate of Seville you will find the tourist information centre of Carmona, a very useful stop as the helpful staff will give you all the information you need to know.

After visiting the Gate of Seville, I would recommend going back to your car and heading to the Gate of Córdoba. The distances are not very long but the steep streets will make it difficult to get to the highest part of the village. You can leave your car around the Gate of Córdoba and then explore the flatter area around, with the Church of Saint Mary, and the square of San Fernando. This can be a good break to have a drink and interact with some locals. Do not miss the Market square either, built after the ecclesiastical confiscation of the convent of Saint Catalina.

Before leaving Carmona you should go the Alcázar of Peter I. As we mentioned, this Alcázar is today a hotel so there is no entrance fee to visit it. If you bring your car, you can park it at the army courtyard before getting into the building. The Alcázar has been transformed after many restorations, but it preserves a very similar appearance in the courtyards and different rooms of the ground floor. At the end you will find the coffee shop with an amazing balcony and wonderful views of the countryside. I would recommend having a coffee in this gorgeous atmosphere. From this point, you will appreciate the importance of the location of Carmona and the privilege of the Alcázar's inhabitants dominating all the lands around. From this balcony you will be able to see the ruins of a series of watchtowers that would communicate through fire with this Alcázar in case of enemies' attacks.

If you wish to stay in Carmona for lunch, you should try Molino de la Romera or La Yedra just beside the Alcázar, with menus consisting of typical Andalusian dishes. Carmona has a lot to offer if you are planning to stay longer, with different convents, churches and noble families' palaces all over the old town.

Osuna

Landmark: Collegiate Church
Distance: 87 kms (54 miles)
Best transport: Train
Public bus: Available
Estimated time: Half or full day

Osuna is a village located in the province of Seville, 87 kms south east of the capital. With a population of about 18,000 inhabitants, it is one of the biggest urban centres of that area of the province.

The origin of Osuna is probably Turdetan, which established a settlement in the 1st millennium BC. This city was then re-founded during the Roman period, becoming an important centre for *Baetica* province. Proof of these splendid times are the remains of the Roman forum, theatre or the Necropolis. From Visigoth and Islamic periods, only a few remains have survived, such as the defensive structure called the Water Tower. In 1240 Osuna was conquered by the troops of the Kingdom of Castile of King Ferdinand III, ending the Muslim period.

The greatest time of the town probably arrived in the 16th century by the hand of the Counts of Ureña that turned Osuna into their noble state capital. The different generations of counts were the patrons of the greatest artists of the Renaissance in Seville, which left in Osuna an impressive monumental heritage with a total of 13 new churches, convents and monasteries, a hospital, the university and the gorgeous Collegiate church built in 1531. In the second half of the 1500s, the Counts received the title of Dukes of Osuna by King Philip II.

The Collegiate Church of Saint Mary of the Assumption represents one of the greatest examples of the Renaissance architecture in Spain. It also hosts works of Baroque masters like

José de Ribera, Martínez Montañés and Juan de Mesa. The Collegiate Church is home to the Family Pantheon of the Dukes, built from 1545, at an attached building located underneath the presbytery. During this period, the University of Osuna was also founded, as proof of its importance. This institution was active from 1548 until 1824. Nowadays the town hosts a university school, linked to the headquarters in Seville. Apart from the Collegiate Church, the Monastery of Encarnación hosts an important collection of sacred art. This former hospital was refurnished in the 1600s in order to host the nuns of the Mercedarias religious order.

Osuna has the privilege of having one of the most beautiful streets in Europe too, according to Unesco. San Pedro Street has the highest concentration of stately noble houses by square metres in the world.

Recommended Itinerary
- Collegiate Church
  - University
  - Monastery of Encarnación
  - San Pedro Street
  - Plaza Mayor
  - Roman Necropolis
  - El coto de las canteras
  - Bullring

Tips & Info
Osuna is still an unknown destination for the greater public, but it offers a lot of possibilities to visitors. Its pleasant and welcoming atmosphere together with its rich historical and artistic heritage will make your stay in Osuna memorable. There are different possibilities to get there. I would recommend taking a train from San Bernardo or Santa Justa station and in a bit more than an hour you will be in Osuna. There are also buses available from Prado de San

Sebastian station and the journey takes approximately 1 hour and 15 minutes. Due to the opening times of the various monuments it is recommended to go to Osuna any day from Tuesday to Sunday.

Once you are in Osuna, you should head to the town centre and visit the tourist information point located in the museum in Sevilla Street. It is highly recommended to purchase the ticket including six monuments (€14 in May 2020). It can be bought at the same Osuna Museum.

After visiting the museum, you can go to Plaza Mayor and then enter the archaeological museum located in the Moorish Water Tower. It will not take you more than half an hour. Continuing your walk, you will get to the monumental area of Osuna. You can start visiting the Monastery of Encarnación, also included with the general ticket and then head to the Collegiate Church.

The Collegiate Church is the archetype of Renaissance in Seville, sharing architect, Diego de Riaño, with the city hall of the capital. The visit includes a guided tour starting every 45-60 minutes (depending on the season).

The third pick of this triangle of astonishing buildings would be the university. The guided tours of the university building and collegiate are strongly recommended not to miss any piece of information. You can get all the information about the starting time at the tourist information office.

The last monument included in the pack is the bullring, only open Saturday, Sunday and on public holidays. The bullring was built at the beginning of the 20th century and has recently become a tourist attraction after appearing in the successful TV series Game of Thrones. On your way to the bullring do not forget to walk along San Pedro Street, the most beautiful street in Europe.

Osuna also hosts an incredible secret spot, called El Coto de las Canteras and popularly known as Andalusia's Petra. These quarries are located in the suburbs of the town, around 15 minutes' walk, and have been in use since the 4th century BC until the 1960s. It shows the perfect combination of natural erosion with the human impact. Nowadays it hosts celebration halls in its interior.

You cannot leave Osuna without enjoying its local gastronomy. It offers a variety of venues where you can stop while you visit the different monuments. Restaurants recommended by Osuna local and licensed guide, Clara Arregui, include La Hospedería del Monasterio, El Casino at Plaza Mayor and Doña Guadalupe. If you are looking for something quicker and lighter, there are good tapas places like Casa Curro, Taberna Jicales or El Molinillo. Osuna is also famous for its local pastries called *aldeanas* that you can get at Confitería Santo Domingo. The nuns of the Conception church also sell their delicious homemade pastries and cakes, do not miss them.

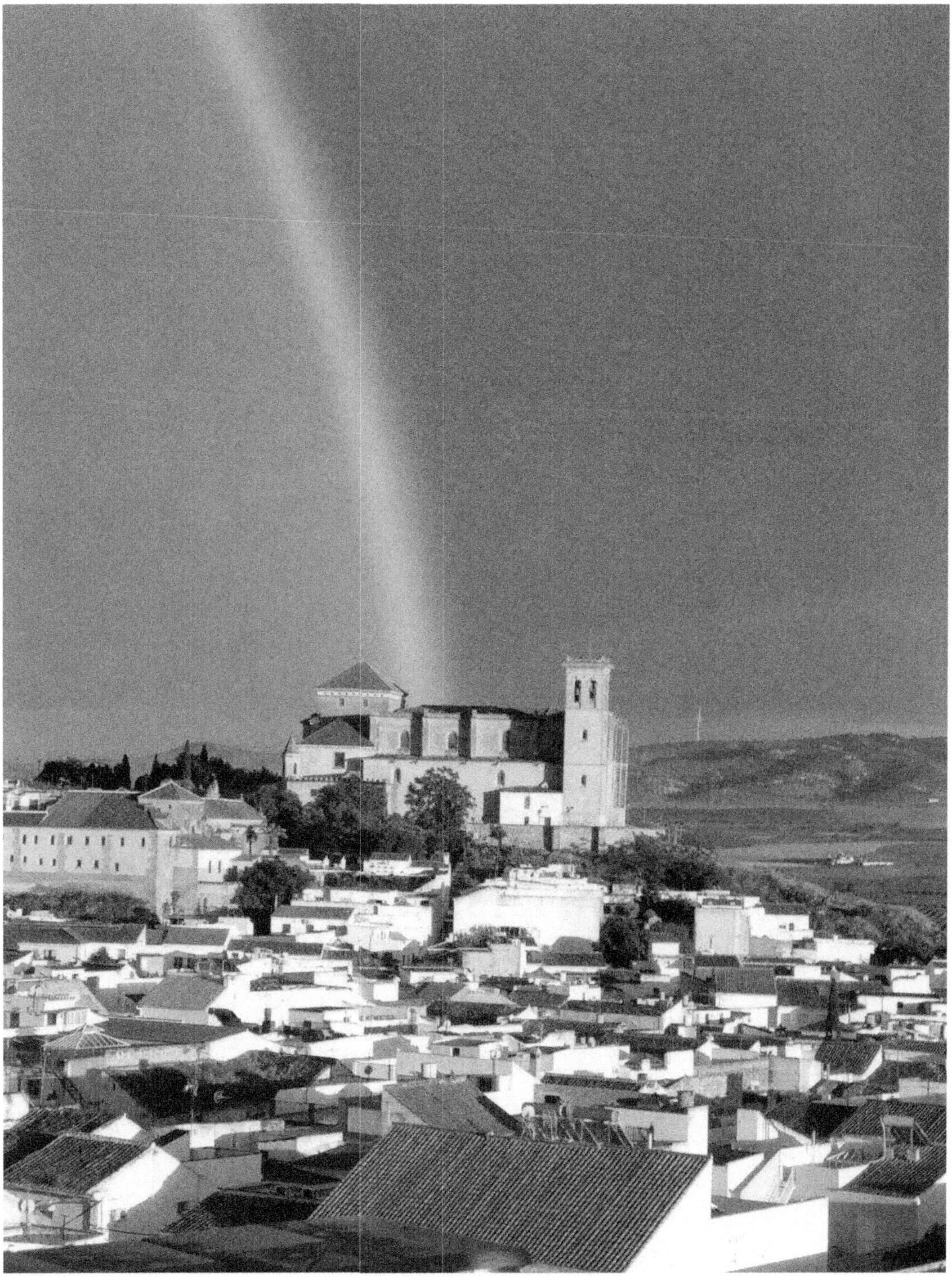

Córdoba

Landmarks: Mosque-Cathedral & Roman Bridge
Distance: 140 kms (87 miles)
Best transport: Train
Public bus: Available
Estimated time: Full day

Córdoba is a city of about 325,000 inhabitants located 140 kms north-east of Seville. The beauty and richness of its monuments have made this city one of the most important tourist destinations in Andalusia. Its historical area was listed as Unesco World Heritage in 1994.

Córdoba was founded in 169 BC by Romans, becoming the capital of the Roman province of Baetica and some important characters of the time were originally from this city, such as the Roman philosopher Seneca. Romans left in Córdoba one of the greatest works of engineering in the Iberian Peninsula; the bridge built around the 1st century AD. With the fall of the Western Roman Empire, Visigoths came to live in the city until the arrival of Muslims in 711 AD.

Córdoba was the capital city of the Independent Ummayad Caliphate from 929 AD to 1031AD, declared by Abderraman III. This status meant the division of the Iberian Peninsula under Moorish rule from the rest of the Muslim world and meant the most glorious time of the city of Córdoba with a population that could have reached 450,000 inhabitants.

The main mosque of the city was finished during this period, even if started by Abderraman I in the 8th century AD. This magnificent structure was built in four different stages. It was the second biggest mosque in the world, only after Mecca, with over 23,000 sq metres. Since the Christian conquest of 1236, it has functioned as a cathedral, but preserves its original appearance in most parts, a never-ending forest of columns and white and red arches made of brick and stone. The *mihrab*, the most sacred part of the mosque, was rebuilt during the third phase of construction with Byzantine mosaics.

Córdoba has a royal palace too, called Alcázar of the Christian Kings, as the original built by Muslims, richer and bigger, was demolished to build this Castilian castle. Close to this palace and the mosque you could also find the former Jewish quarter of Córdoba with some medieval remains as the *zoco*(market) and the synagogue, one of the three medieval synagogues preserved in Spain. Córdoba is also famous for its patios, decorated with colourful flowers.

Recommended Itinerary
- Roman Bridge
- Alcázar de los Reyes Cristianos
- Patios
- Jewish quarter
- Synagogue
- Mosque-Cathedral

Tips & Info
Córdoba is a must see for everybody visiting Andalusia. Even if you are not thinking of staying there during your trip, you should consider organising a full day trip to this magnificent city.

Córdoba is very well connected with Seville by train and the AVE (fast train) will get you there in only 40 minutes from Santa Justa station. There are other cheaper options with slower trains too; you will have plenty of options for a round trip in a single day.

Once you are in Córdoba, you must head to the city centre and you will be around the monumental area in just 15 or 20 minutes' walk. You can start your visit by Calahorra tower and the Roman Bridge. This was the only access to the city from the south until the 20th century and throughout history, the only weak point for its defence. That is why Calahorra tower was reinforced by the different civilisations that lived in the city. By walking on the Roman Bridge, you will see the sculpture of Archangel Saint Raphael, the protector of the city, very present in many churches. According to the legend, Saint Raphael saved the city of Córdoba from the plague.

You can continue your walk heading to the Alcázar. The Alcázar of Córdoba is probably not as impressive as the Alcázar in Seville, but it is still worthy of a visit. The ticket costs €4.50 and you can visit it in a bit more than an hour. This is the palace where Cristopher Colombus first presented his project to Queen Isabella and King Ferdinand in January 1486.

I would highly recommend visiting the patio of the Association of Patios of Córdoba in Calle San Basilio. It is well maintained all year round and its workers will only ask for a tip to visit. The festival of patios in Córdoba takes place in May and private house owners will open their gates to show them to visitors and participate in the contest.

Wandering the streets of the former Jewish quarter is an experience you cannot miss while in Córdoba. The Jewish quarter was active after the Christian conquest of 1236 until the definite expulsion of 1492. An important Jewish character was born in this city, Maimonides and developed his work as a doctor, philosopher and astronomer during the Muslim rule. The synagogue is a must-see too. It was built during the 1300s and then converted into a Christian church.

The highlight of your stay in Córdoba must be the visit to the Mosque-Cathedral. The ticket to get in has a price of €10 with concessions for children, students and retired visitors and can be purchased directly at the ticket office located in the Orange Trees Courtyard.

I highly recommend visiting the Mosque-Cathedral with a licensed guide. Not every guide recognised by the cultural department of the government of Andalusia can guide groups inside the Mosque as they need a special credential. You can contact any in advance and arrange a guided visit. The other possibility is getting the audio guide at the stand next to the ticket office. I would not recommend that you do so as inside the Mosque, there are no signs with numbers to follow the visit and you would not even know what you are looking at. The standard visit to the Mosque-Cathedral is a bit more than an hour.

The gastronomy is another strong point of a visit to Córdoba. There are two dishes you cannot miss that are *salmorejo*, a cold tomato soup and *flamenquín*, a rolled cordon bleu. You will have them served in every place, like the lovely tavern *El Abanico*, beside the mosque or by the riverside in *La Taberna del Río*.

Ronda & the White Villages

Landmarks: Zahara, Setenil & Ronda
Distance: 130 kms (80 miles)
Best transport: Private car
Public bus: Available (To Ronda)
Estimated time: Full day

The White Villages of Cádiz province, as well as Ronda in Málaga, are some of the most attractive tourist destinations and very popular among visitors looking to discover rural Andalusia. The geography of these areas as well as the historical importance of these towns made them preserve a rich artistic heritage apart from its unique natural landscapes.

Zahara de la Sierra is located 100 kms (62 miles) from Seville in the Natural Park of Sierra de Grazalema, at about 500 metres above sea level on top of a hill. Zahara has about 1,300 inhabitants that live mainly from livestock and agriculture. Zahara is home to one of those castles that served as a fortress, and worked as a border between Christian and Muslim Kingdoms for over 250 years.

Setenil de las Bodegas is another mandatory stop in a journey through theWhite Villages. Setenil is 121 kms(75 miles) from Seville and 32 kms (20 miles) from Zahara. Setenil is crossed by Trejo River gorge and it is unique because of the houses built along the gorge into the rock walls. The main streets built at the gorge get the names of *Cuevas de la sombra* (caves of the shade) and *Cuevas del sol* (caves of the sun). Setenil is famous for its livestock products, with Iberian meat production still the main occupation for some of the 2,700 inhabitants of the village.

Ronda is considered more a city than a village with about 35,000 inhabitants. The capital of the mountains of Malaga province is 132 kms (82 miles) from the centre of Seville. Ronda is a very popular tourist destination due to its unique geography and rich history.

Ronda consists of two hills divided by an impressive natural canyon of over 100 metres deep that has historically needed to be crossed. First Romans, then Muslims and finally Spaniards in the 18th century built bridges that connected both areas at different highs.

Historically, Ronda was one of the last cities to be conquered by Christians from the Muslims and only surrendered in 1485. This city, as an administrative capital of the area, also boasts a rich artistic heritage in its churches, convents, palaces and defensive walls. The bullring of Ronda is considered one of the oldest in Spain, built in 1785. It hosts a bullfight museum.

Recommended Itinerary
- Viewpoint of Zahara de la Sierra
- Zahara castle
- Setenil de las Bodegas
- Bullring (Ronda)
- Romantic Travellers' Park (Ronda)
- Parador of Ronda
- New bridge of Ronda
- Old town of Ronda
- Arab baths of Ronda

Tips & Info

Getting to the White Villages is not an easy task for a tourist. Public transport is not widely available and many visitors would book a day trip with any company in order to visit as much as possible. Only Ronda can be reached by bus from Seville. The best way to fully enjoy a trip to this area would be to rent a private car, and drive through these countryside roads.

On your way there, you can stop at the Castle of Aguzaderas, located in El Coronil and built by Moorish in the 1300s. Once in Zahara, you should stop by the viewpoint at the entrance of the village with an amazing view of the castle and the dam made in the

Guadalete River. After a short walk around the village you will be ready to visit the castle, but be aware that the way up can be a bit difficult and steep. The view from the top though is well worth it.

Back to your car, you can head to the next destination, Setenil de las Bodegas. On your way there you will see fields of olive and cork trees and farms dedicated to Iberian pork meats. In Setenil, it is better to park at the highest part of the village and walk down enjoying the different images of the gorge. Once you get to the lowest part, do not miss the opportunity to visit any of the taverns or shops built into the rock.

In about 25 minutes from Setenil you should get to Ronda, where your first duty would be finding a parking spot. My recommendation is leaving your car near the bus station or in any of the private car parks. Go for a walk in the Alameda Park, where you will first see the height of the Tajo canyon. This park is connected with the bullring. If you decide to visit it, the ticket costs €8 and you can get an audio guide for €1.50 extra. Continuing your walk along the canyon, you will get to the Romantic Travellers' Park, dedicated to those first European visitors that came to the area in the 1800s and showed the beauty of these villages through their writings and paintings. Getting to the new bridge, you will see the Parador, the former city hall now converted into a hotel at the most privileged location in the whole city. The new bridge is the most impressive image of Ronda; probably not by crossing it, but by looking at it from the bottom. To do so, you will have to cross it to the old part of the city and take the path down that will bring you to the bottom of the canyon. Only from there will you appreciate how magnificent this bridge is. Back up, you can go for a walk along the narrow streets of old Ronda, visit the Arab baths, the Gate of Almocábar or the different stately noble palaces around.

Ronda is a place where you could stay for more than a day and if you do so, you will have the chance of trying some of the best meals and wines from this area. Apart from the Parador restaurant, I would recommend *Pedro Romero* restaurant or *El Lechuguita* close to the bullring and *Mesón Carmen* in the old town. Across the street from the bullring you will see one of the biggest hotels in Ronda called Catalonia. I strongly recommend going to the rooftop terrace for a drink or coffee around sunset.

If it is time to go back to Seville, it will take you about 1.5 hours to get back to the capital and you will probably be very tired, but with new experiences and amazing places discovered. Apart from the villages mentioned here, there are other lovely places to stop like Grazalema, Olvera, or Arcos de la Frontera, in case you prefer to organise an alternative route.

FAQ

Before arrival

- *What is the best area to look for accommodation in Seville?*

In Seville all the interesting places are within walking distance, so anywhere inside the former historical walls (city centre) or Triana should work fine.

- *My accommodation is not in the city centre. What is the transport in Seville like?*

Buses in Seville connect every part of the city with the city centre. Please check the bus number you should take and commuting time to get to the city centre before arrival. Seville also has one metro line that is very convenient if you are staying along it.

- *What is the best way to get to the city centre from the airport? Should I book a transfer?*

There is a bus running every 20 minutes and connecting the airport with the city centre in about 40 minutes. The bus has no number, but it is called EA and it costs €4 (one way) and €6 (return). The streets of the city centre are narrow and buses do not enter the monumental area, so you will probably have to walk after. A taxi from the airport costs about €25.

- *What is the weather like in Seville?*

Seville is a warm city; please check the forecast before arrival. Bring sunscreen if you are visiting in summer and protect yourself from the sun from 12pm to 5pm.

- *Is Seville safe for tourists?*

Seville is a very quiet city and totally safe for visitors. Only in places like *Plaza de España* you should be careful as the police sometimes advise that there are pickpockets around.

- *I get to Seville in the morning and my accommodation will not be available until 3 pm. Where can I leave my luggage?*

You can first check with your Airbnb host or hotel. Most of the tourist information and tours companies offer the locker service too. Please contact them in advance.

- *Are tips common after good service?*

Tips are never mandatory in Spain and they will not be included in the price you pay. If you feel you have received a good service, you can always give a tip. There is no minimum or percentage.

- *I have no idea of Spanish, will I be in trouble?*

Seville city centre has changed a lot in the past few years and most restaurants and cultural interest sites will have translations in English. With locals, the level of English is improving but there is still a lot to do in order to become a bilingual society. Most people will know the basics to communicate and that should be enough for you to understand.

- *I will be visiting during Holy Week. What should I expect?*

Holy Week means that there will be a huge amount of people around the streets of the city centre and the first rule is not to become overwhelmed. It may be difficult for you to get to your accommodation due to the different processions. Please check with your hotel or Airbnb host for the best time to get to your accommodation, mainly on your first day as you will be carrying your luggage.

- **I will be visiting during the April Fair. What should I expect?**

The April Fair does not take place all over the city but at a specific enclosure and it should not affect your stay in Seville. Timetables of certain locations and shops will change but regarding transport you will have more availability as they work 24/7.

- **I plan not to bring a lot of cash; can I pay by card everywhere?**

Most places around the city accept payments with debit/credit cards. In some of these places there will be a minimum charge of €10 to do so, due to the fact that the commission to the bank in Spain is not paid by the customer but by the bar/restaurant owner. In some places *American Express* cards are not accepted. Please check with your bank before arrival.

- **My phone company does not include a data bundle abroad. Where can I get a prepaid sim card?**

In Spain there are three main phone companies: Orange, Movistar andVodafone. You can check in any of their shops about the fares for short stays in order to get a Spanish number.

On site

- **What are the usual lunch/dinner times for locals?**

Spaniards eat late and you will feel it as soon as you get here. A normal lunch time is between 2.30pm and 3.30pm, while dinner is usually after 9.30pm.

- **What times do shops open and close?**

It will depend on the type of shop, but opening times are usually between 9.30am and 10am and closing time around 10pm. Some of the shops will close for lunch/siesta break from 2pm to 4/5pm.

- **I want to eat tapas. How many should I order?**

Tapas in Seville are usually bigger than in other parts of northern Spain. Do not order more than two or three tapas per person for a whole lunch or dinner.

- **I am visiting in summer. Does business work as usual?**

During July and August lots of companies will change their standard schedule and that can happen as well with offices and shops, but it should not affect tourist attractions.

- **Can I go shopping every day?**

Shops in Seville (including supermarkets) close on Sundays and on public holidays. There are only a few souvenir shops and small supermarkets open on Sundays. Please take this into consideration when planning your stay in Seville.

- **What time does public transport open and close?**

Buses usually run from 6am until midnight. Depending where in the city you are staying, there will be some night buses working until 4am. The metro line runs from 6.30am until 11pm, but closes at 2am on Fridays and Saturdays.

- **Where can I rent a car?**

Most of the car rental companies will have an office at Santa Justa Station and that would be the most convenient place to go.

- ***What do locals have for breakfast?***

In Seville locals usually get a salty breakfast consisting of toast with olive oil, tomato and Iberian ham with a coffee (café con leche) or orange juice.

- ***What time do monuments usually close?***

The main monuments close at about 5.30pm during the winter months and 7pm in summer. All this information is described in previous chapters of this book.

- ***I want to go out at night. Which area should I go to?***

There are different party areas around the city centre. For a drink I would recommend Paseo de Colón, Alameda or Alfalfa. Regarding night clubs, the biggest and most popular is called *Uthopia* and it is located in Plaza de Armas. In summer there are some outdoors clubs too like *Líbano*, *Casino* or *Bilindo*.

- ***I have an emergency and need to see a doctor. Where should I go?***

If you have medical insurance, contact them for information. If you do not, you can go to any of the hospitals close to the city centre, *Virgen del Rocío* hospital or *Virgen Macarena* hospital.

Printed in Great Britain
by Amazon